Lam Nguyen

Cracking the Python

An Introduction to Computer Programming

Preface

It is noted that Computer Programming, also known as Software Engineering, is always ranked among top jobs in America. That's why Computer Science has become favorite major of many people. As a programmer, I realize that the sooner you code, the more familiar and better you get in computer programming. Therefore, this book is well designed for learners at all ages ranged from middle or high school students to adults who want to learn coding as it does not assume any prior background in computer programming. Python is chosen as the programming language used in this book as I believe it is suitable and convenient for all beginners to start learning computer programming. If you are an absolute beginner, this book is the right choice for you to step into the world of Computer Science. If you are an experienced learner, this book brings you to an interesting journey to Python discovery.

All the topics are selectively chosen and effectively placed in a rational order that helps the learner can become hero from zero. It starts by introducing you to data types in programming as well as their features and then guides you to more advanced topics. In this book, examples are vividly demonstrated to help you understand deeply the lessons, and exercises are designed to strengthen your knowledge. Instead of talking too much to explain a topic by numerous words, this book shows you different examples and exercises to make you think, deeply think and imagine how the programs work. That is how the book works.

Acknowledgements

I would like to thank my friend Minh, who introduced me to the wonderful world of Computer Science. I would also like to thank all my professors at Luther College for having endowed me with their tremendous knowledge. I would not have made it without them. I am extremely grateful to my good friend, Clinton Akomea-Agyin, who has tirelessly walked by my side during this arduous journey. Finally, I would like to thank my students who gave me motivation to write this book, a book, I believe, that empowers not only my students but also the young generation.

Trademarks

All trademarks are acknowledged as belonging to their respective companies.

Contact Information

I would love to hear from you. For feedback or suggestions, you can contact me at nguyenhunglam.sg@gmail.com

Good Things Start Here...

Table of Contents

CHAPTER 1: INTRO TO PYTHON

• What is Python?

Like Java, C++ or many others, Python is a programming language. In real life, people communicate by many languages such as English, Spanish, French, Chinese or Vietnamese. Similarly, programmers "communicate" with computer by different languages such as Java, C#, Ruby or Python. In my opinion, I would say Python is just like English because of its simplicity and popularity.

Python is an ideal first language for beginner to learn and a good start for anyone who wants to become a Computer Scientist. Python, an interpreted programming language, is designed to emphasize code readability because it does not require lots of curly braces to delimit code blocks like other languages do. Additionally, Python syntax also allows programmers to express concepts in fewer lines of code than might be used in other languages such as Java or C#. Python also has many standard libraries available supporting to write some very interesting programs. A library is simply a collection of source codes pre-written that we can use for our programs.

● Installing Python:

To run a Python code, you need a Python interpreter. Python interpreter is a program that reads a Python code and executes the statement written in it. When you have your code written, Python interpreter will help you execute your Python code to see what your work does. This is like when you record a song, the MP3 player helps you to listen what you recorded. In other words, Python interpreter plays the same role as a MP3 player helps you play your songs.

To "listen to your song", you must have Python installed on your computer first. Python is free and available for download on web. There were some changes to the Python programming language from Python 2 to Python 3 within the last few years. In this book, we will install and work on Python 3, the most updated one.

To install Python, if you have a Mac, then Python is already installed. To check the version, start the Terminal window and type *python*. If you are running Windows, you can get the installation package on https://www.python.org/

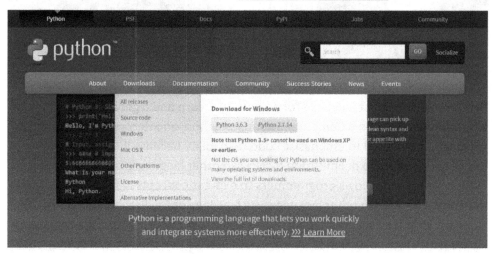

Click on Python 3.6.3 (Python 3) to download it then you will have the package to install. Besides, to have more details which version you need to get, click on *View the full list of downloads*, you can pick the right version on the list shown below:

Python >>> Downloads >>> Windows

Python Releases for Windows

- Latest Python 3 Release - Python 3.6.3
- Latest Python 2 Release - Python 2.7.14

- Python 3.6.3 - 2017-10-03
  - Download Windows x86 web-based installer
  - Download Windows x86 executable installer
  - Download Windows x86 embeddable zip file
  - Download Windows x86-64 web-based installer
  - Download Windows x86-64 executable installer
  - Download Windows x86-64 embeddable zip file
  - Download Windows help file
- Python 3.7.0a1 - 2017-09-19
  - Download Windows x86 web-based installer
  - Download Windows x86 executable installer
  - Download Windows x86 embeddable zip file
  - Download Windows x86-64 web-based installer
  - Download Windows x86-64 executable installer
  - Download Windows x86-64 embeddable zip file
  - Download Windows help file

After having your package downloaded, double click to open the .exe file and install it like many other programs:

Now, you need an editor to type your code and run your Python programs conveniently. An editor designed for writing codes is called an IDE, which stands for Integrated Development Environment. IDE supports highlighting, indentation, hints and key words, besides helping your program run straight from the editor. To work with Python programs, I recommend you to use Wing IDE, which is available for Microsoft Windows, Mac OS X, and Linux. Significantly, Wing IDE also includes an integrated debugger, allowing you to run your code, stop at some points, and inspect the state of your program to help you better understand the flow of code when it gets executed.

You can run Python programs without an IDE, but you need an IDE to write your programs conveniently and understand more how your Python programs work through debugging. This is like you can cook rice without the rice cooker, but everything is easy and handy to cook rich with a rice cooker. To install Wing IDE, you need to download it from https://wingware.com/downloads

Wing Pro seems has more characteristics than other two options. However, Wing 101 is good enough for us to start learning coding with Python without paying for a license. Pick the appropriate version for your computer and download it.

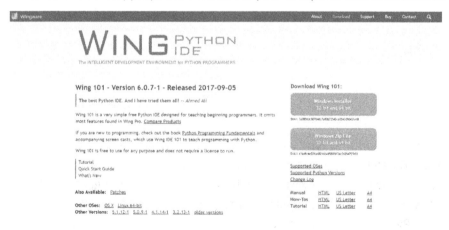

If you use Mac, pick the Mac version. On the other hand, if you are trying to install on Windows, pick the Windows version.

Next, double click on the .exe file to open and install it as usual:

Click Next and start installing, and then click Finish when it is completed.

To recapitulate, everything is all set when we finish downloading and installing Python from https://www.python.org and Wing IDE 101 from https://wingware.com. Now, we are ready for learning and working with Python.

CHAPTER 2: BASICS OF PYTHON

• Data Types:

Data types are used to classify different kinds of value in programming. There are many types of data, but in this chapter, we just introduced 4 basic data types which are String, Integer, Float and Boolean. We will learn and understand more about them via examples rather than theoretical definitions.

o String

Anything covered by the quotation marks is called *String*.

Examples:

"hello"

"12345"

"ab23nfg874@#$%"

All of examples above are *String* as they are clearly covered by quotation marks.

o Integer

Integers are whole numbers, which are not fractions.

Examples:

0

1

-8

987654321

❖ Quick Question:

"25" is a *String* or *Integer* ?

    A) String

    B) Integer

✓ A is the correct answer. No matter what it is inside the quotation marks, anything covered by quotation marks is *String*.

o **Float**

Decimal numbers, which are not whole numbers, in Python are called *Float*.

Examples:

3.14

-2.1

2.0

o **Boolean**

Boolean is a value of True or False.

Examples:

True

False

✍ *Check Your Understanding:*

Match the values on the left side with their appropriate types on the right side.

1) 4.5	A) String
2) "6"	B) Integer
3) 7	C) Float
4) False	D) Boolean

4.5 is a decimal number, so its type is *float.* "6" is a *String* because the number is covered by quotation marks. 7 is *Integer* as it is clearly a whole number. Finally, False is a *Boolean* value.

• Print & Comment Stuffs:

In Python, **Print** is a command asking to display the output. Things are supposed to be printed are placed inside the parentheses.

The blank space in Python does not really affect the code, unless it is inside the quotation mark.

For example:

```
print("Hello World")
print    ("White Space doesn't matter"    )
print("  White Space MATTERS       NOW")
print(25)
```

Output:

```
Hello World
White Space doesn't matter
  White Space MATTERS      NOW
25
```

It can be easily seen that 4 lines of output display 4 print statements we wrote before. The first simply prints out Hello World. The second and third print statements show us how blank spaces affect the code. As long as blank spaces are outside the quotation marks, they won't affect the output. However, the output prints out exactly every blank space we put in the quotation marks as above.

Sometimes, printing stuffs is tricky.

```
print(2+3)
print("2+3")
```

Output:

```
5
2+3
```

In the first line, we want to print 2 + 3, so Python will understand it as a math expression and will compute the result for us. That's why the output is 5 as 2 + 3 equals 5. However, in the second line, 2 + 3 now is covered by the quotation marks. So "2+3" is a *String*, and the program will print out exactly what's covered by the quotation marks.

Now, let's look at another printing example and guess what the output will be before looking at the answer:

```
print("2+3=",2+3)
```

Output:

```
2+3=5
```

The comma separates the printing stuffs into 2 parts: the first part is "2+3=" and the second part is 2+3. For the first part, "2+3=" will give the output exactly as 2+3= like previous examples, while 2 + 3 will compute the result as 5. Thus, combined by two parts, the output is 2+3=5.

On the other hand, In Python, # is the symbol used for comments in the code. In other words, comments (which started by # does not affect the code at all).

Example:

```
#This is what I wanna show you.
#Comments does not affect the code at all.
print("This is it.")
#You see?
```

Output:

```
This is it.
```

The symbol # is not necessary always at the beginning of lines. It can also be at anywhere in the line. For example:

```
print(5) #This is the number 5

print("5")#This is a String.
```

Output:

```
5

5
```

As you can clearly see, the comments put in the code doesn't affect or change the output supposed to be. These comments even play a role as an explanation next to the coding lines.

Besides #, triple quotes (3 single quotes) also can be used for commenting many lines in the code by different ways. For example:

```
''' this is just a comment

it is not finished yet

this comment includes many lines

now we gonna close this comment

'''

print("Hello World")
```

Output

```
Hello World
```

• Types & Controls:

We have studied types of data and printing stuffs so far. Now it's time to check if the Python understands exactly what we understood before. To check a type of a data, we use the command **type**. For example.

```
print(type(5))
print(type("5"))
print(type(5.0))
print(type(True))
```

Output:

```
<class 'int'>
<class 'str'>
<class 'float'>
<class 'bool'>
```

The output looks like that what we have learned so far about data types in Python make sense and they can be shown by printing. **Type** is the command used for checking data type. It can be seen that 'int' stands for Integer; 'str' stands for String; 'float' stands for float numbers and 'bool' stands for Boolean. <class 'int'> indicates that 5 belongs to class Integer in Python. Same things with other data types.

```
print(type('This is a string.') )
print(type("this is also a string.") )
print(type("""string again.""") )
print(type('''still a string...''') )
```

Output:

```
<class 'str'>
<class 'str'>
<class 'str'>
<class 'str'>
```

It is noted that data type can be transformed from one to another. Type conversion helps us to solve problems in some situations. Here are ways of type conversion:

Converse to String	⇨	str(something)
Converse to Integer	⇨	int(something)
Converse to Float	⇨	float(something)
Converse to Boolean	⇨	bool(something)

♦ Examples:

▪ Type conversion between Float and Integer:

```
print(3.14, int(3.14))
print(3.9, int(3.9))
print(3, float(3))
```

Output

```
3.14 3
3.9 3
3 3.0
```

From the code above, we can see every print line has two parts: the original data and the data after conversion. In line 1 and 2, both Float numbers 3.14 and 3.9 became 3 when it is conversed to Integer. Therefore, no matter how close 3.9 is to 4, it is never rounded up but down to the nearest integer. On the other hand, an Integer 3 become 3.0, a float number with the same value as 3.

- Type conversion To String:

```
print(type(7))
print(str(7))
print(type(str(7)))
```

Output:

```
<class 'int'>
7
<class 'str'>
```

It is clear that the type of 7 is Integer, so the first line of output makes sense. The second line of output is 7, but this 7 is not an integer anymore. The command str(7) conversed an Integer to a String. The last line of the output confirm the type of 7 after conversed to String. It showed us after the conversion to String, the type of 7 now is 'str' instead of 'int'.

Another example from Float to String:

```
print(type(14.12))
print(str(14.12))
print(type(str(14.12)))
```

Output:

```
<class 'float'>
14.12
<class 'str'>
```

Similarly, 14.12 is a Float, while str(14.12) is a String. The output can blind us sometimes cause 14.12 (at line 2) in this case looks like a Float, but it was actually conversed to String.

- Conversion from a String to a Number

A String can become a number through conversion, and this is one of the most powerful and useful tool in dealing with input from users.

```
print("1412")

print(type("1412"))

print(int(1412))

print(type(int(1412)))
```

Output:

```
1412

<class 'str'>

1412

<class 'int'>
```

1412 appears twice in the output. However, the former one is a String, while the latter one is an Integer in this code. Two print lines to check the types already confirmed the difference between these two 1412s.

Is it true that a String can always be transformed to a number?

```
print("Hello")

print(int("Hello"))
```

Output:

```
ValueError: invalid literal for int() with base 10: 'Hello' on line 1
```

In this case, error happens as "Hello" can never a number. This is clear.

- Conversion with Boolean:

Let's take a look at the first example of conversion to Boolean:

```
print("True")

print(type("True"))

print(bool("True"))

print(type(bool("True")))
```

Output:

```
True

<class 'str'>

True

<class 'bool'>
```

The second line and the fourth line seems similar. However, their types are different. The first one is a String as it is covered by quotation marks. The second one is a Boolean expression, which can be confirmed by the last line of output.

How about if we want to converse something else that is not "True" to a Boolean?

```
print("Hello")

print(bool("Hello"))

print(56)

print(bool(56))

print(bool("False"))
```

Output:

```
Hello
True
56
True
True
```

This output is kind of surprising as all of the data conversed to Boolean now become True. Noticeably, even the last data which is a String "False" still become True when it is conversed to a Boolean expression.

• Variables & Controls:

In Python programming, a variable is a memory location which has a name and contains some information referred to as a value. Values can be String, Integers, and others. Variables must be assigned before being referenced.

Some important things to remember about the name of a variable:

- A variable's name cannot contain blank spaces.
- Names are Case-Sensitive.
- Must begin with a letter or underscore (_).
- Letters, numbers, and underscore can be used in naming a variable.
- Underscores, however, placed at the beginning of the name have some special meanings, so start all names with a letter for safe reasons.

We use the equal sign (=) to assign a value to a variable.

How to declare a variable:

```
nameOfVariable = itsInformation
```

For example:

```
myWords = "Hello World"
aNum = 15
print(myWords)
print(aNum)
```

Output:

```
Hello World
15
```

The output is supposed to print out *myWords* and *aNum* because of last two lines in the code. They are not String as they are not covered by quotation marks. They are not numbers or Boolean expressions neither. So what will be printed out is different from what we learned before. They are variables and they carry values. Look at the first two lines we can see myWords carry a value, which a String "Hello World", and aNum carry the value of 15. That's why when we try to print *myWords* and *aNum*, "Hello World" and 15 are printed out.

Let's try one more example:

```
a = "hello"
b = 4
c = 2.7
print(type(a))
print(type(b))
print(type(c))
```

Output:

```
<class 'str'>

<class 'int'>

<class 'float'>
```

As a, b, and c carry values, their types are actually their values' types. Therefore, a is a String because "hello" is a String; b is an Integer as 4 is an Integer; c is float number just like 2.7.

Next, let's take a look at another example below:

```
a = 2

b = 3

print(a+b)
```

Output:

```
5
```

2 and 3 are assigned to a and b respectively, so a + b is actually 2 + 3. That's why 5 is the output we expect to see.

✎ Quick Question:

What is printed when the code below executes?

```
x = "hello"

x = 3.14

x = 35

print(x)
```

A) hello
B) 3.14
C) 35
D) Error

✓ C is the Correct Answer. The variable x contains the last value assigned to it when it is printed.

• Operators:

Operators are special tokens used for computations

o 4 basic Arithmetic operators:

+	Addition
-	Subtraction
*	Multiplication
/	Division

First, let's take a look at how these 4 basic Arithmetic operators work in Python.

```
print( 7 + 2 )
print( 7 - 2 )
print( 7 * 2 )
print( 7 / 2 )
```

Output:

```
9
5
14
3.5
```

Similar to Math, Python understands that 7+2=9, 7-2=5, 7*2=14, and 7/2=3.5.

o Additional useful operators in Python:

**	Exponentiation (Power)
//	Divide and then round down to the nearest integer
%	Mod (Take remainder after division)

This code will help you understand more about these new operators:

```
print(7**2)

print(7//2)

print(7%2)
```

Output:

```
49

3.0

1
```

As you can see, 7**2 means 7^2 = 49. 7 // 2 means 7 / 2 = 3.5 and 3.5 is rounded down to 3, which is the nearest integer (it is never rounded up to). Finally, in Math, 7 / 2 = 3 and remainder is 1, so 7 % 2 will give us 1 as the result.

✎ Quick Question:

Think about and predict what the output will be if the code below is executed:

```
x = 28

y = 5

print( x % y )

print( x / 5 )

print(x // 5 )
```

Your answer:

....

//Think about the output before checking the answer below

```
3
5.6
5
```

From the code, x equals to 28 and y equals to 5. We have 28 % 5 = 3 because 3 is the remainder in this integer division. Besides, 25 / 5 = 5.6 and 5.6 can be rounded down to 5 if we use the integer division operator (//). Thus, 3, 5.6, and 5 are 3 results we expect in the output.

❖ Order of Operations:
- Python follows the same precedence rules that mathematics does.
- Parentheses have the highest precedence.
- Exponentiation has the next highest precedence.
- Multiplication (*) and division (/) have the same precedence, and addition (+) and subtraction (-) have the same precedence.
- Multiplication and division have higher precedence than addition and subtraction.
- Operators with the same precedence (except for exponentiation) are evaluated from left-to-right. It's known as left-associative.
- Only exponentiation (**) follows right-associative.

Examples:

```
print(27 - 2 * 7 // 2 + 7)
```

Output:

```
27
```

From the code above, applying multiplication precedence and left-associative rule, we calculate 2 * 7 =14 first, then 14 // 2 = 7. Next, from the left we have 27 – 7 = 20. Finally, 20 + 7 = 27. The output is 27.

Let's take a look at an example of exponentiation to see how we use right-associative:

```
print(3 ** 2 ** 3)
print((3 ** 2) ** 3)
```

Output:

```
6561
729
```

If we follow the left-associative rule for the first line, we will get $3^2 = 9$, and then $9^3 = 729$. However, Python follows the right-associative rule for exponentiation. So it calculates $2^3 = 8$ first, and then $3^8 = 6561$. If we want to calculate 3^2 first, we have to use parentheses like the second line because parentheses have the highest precedence.

🐾 Check Your Understanding

1) What is the value of the following expression:

$$3 - 4 + 7 * 5 // 3 - (5 + 2)$$

A) 7
B) 3
C) 6
D) 9

2) What is the value of the following expression:

$$2 ** 2 ** 3 * 3$$

A) 1024
B) 768
C) 512
D) 192

✓ Answer:

1) B

As parentheses have the highest precedence, 5+2=7 is calculated first. Then multiplication and division should be evaluated next based on left-associative rule. So 7*5 = 35, then 35 // 3 = 11. Finally, from the left to right 3-4+11-7 = 3.

2) B

As exponentiation has the higher precedence than the multiplication has, we evaluate the exponentiation first. Because we have two exponentiation operators, we calculate from the right to the left. Therefore 2 ** 3 = 2^3 = 8, then 2^8 = 256. Finally, 256 * 3 = 768.

o Relational Operators

==	equal
!=	not equal
>	greater than
<	less than
>=	greater than or equal
<=	less than or equal

(*) Notice: == (double signs) means equal, but = just means assigning values.

Let's check how these relational operators work through the following example:

```
print(5<7)
print(5<=7)
print(5==7)
print(5!=7)
print(5>7)
print(5>=7)
```

Output:

```
True

True

False

True

False

False
```

The output says it all. 5 is definitely less than 7 and not equal 7. That's why 5 < 7, 5 <= 7, and 5 != 7 are True. 5 > 7, 5 >=7, and 5 == 7 are False.

o   Logical Operators by Words

not	not
and	and (check both conditions are True)
or	either or (check at least 1 of them is True)

Example:

```
print(not(5 > 7))

print(5 > 7 and 7 > 5)

print(5 > 7 or 7 > 5)
```

Output:

```
True

False

True
```

It's clear that 5 > 7 is False, so **not** False is True. In other words, it's True that there is no fact that 5 > 7. In the second line, the keyword **and** requires two statements must be True. That's why the output is False because 5 > 7 is False even though 7 > 5 is True. Finally, 5 > 7 or 7 > 5 is True because the key word **or** requires just one of them (7 > 5) is True.

• Updating Variables:

As we learned before, a variable contains the last value assigned to it when it is printed. After gaining a bunch of knowledge of operators, let's discover how to update and control variables through operation.

First, let's take a look at a very simple example of updating variable with addition operator:

```
x = 2
x = x + 5
print(x)
```

Output:

```
7
```

At first, 2 was assigned to x, so x equals 2. After that, we added 5 to the initial value (2), so the new x was updated. Now x equals 2 + 5 =7. That's why 7 is our final output because it the most updated x in this code.

Another example:

```
a = 2
a = a + 2
a = a * 2
a = a -2
```

```
print(a)
```

Output:

```
6
```

The value of a started at 2. After that, it increased by 2 to become 4, and then doubled itself to reach 8. Finally, 8 − 2 = 6, and 6 is our final answer for the output.

✎ Check Your Understanding:

What is printed when the following statements execute?

```
y = 5
y = y − 2
y = y ** 2
print( y == 5 )
```

A) 9
B) 5
C) False
D) True

✓ Answer:

C is the correct answer. The value of y started at 5 at the beginning, then changed to 3 after subtraction by 2, and finally become 9 as $3^2 = 9$. So 9 is the most updated value of y, but it's not the answer. The print statement asked you if 9 is equal 5 or not (notice the double equal signs). 9 never equals to 5, so the output is False.

• Input:

Instead of deciding data values for your program, sometimes you need to ask users for values they want to put in. For example, in real life, it is very common that users type their names as well as their information to sign up for accounts on websites, so it is clear that you cannot decide those values and need to get information from the users. Therefore, getting input from users plays an important role in programming. To get input from the user, you can use the *input()* function. When the input() function is called, it allows the user to decide and type the information they want to put in the program.

To be more detailed, when the function is called, the prompt is shown to ask the user what to put in. For example, if you want a random number from user, you should write n = input("Enter a number: "). "Enter a number" is the prompt that will be shown to the user. After that, when the user enter the number and press enter, the information that has been entered will be returned from the input function, and assigned to the variable *n*. We can try this with this example:

```
n = input("Enter a number: ")
print("The number you put in: ", n)
```

When you run this code, you will see:

If you type 5 and then enter, the output will be:

```
Debug I/O    Python Shell    Messages    OS Commands
Debug I/O (stdin, stdout, stderr) appears below
Enter a number: 5
The number you put in:   5
```

After running the program, the user will see a message "Enter a number: " from the computer. Putting 5 and pressing enter keyboard, the line "The number you put in: 5" is shown as a result.

Now, is 5 here really an integer?

```
n = input("Enter a number: ")
print(type(n))
```

Ouput:

```
Debug I/O    Python Shell    Messages    OS Commands

Debug I/O (stdin, stdout, stderr) appears below

Enter a number: 5
<class 'str'>
```

The output says it all. The number 5 that we got from the user is a String, not an Integer as it looks. This is because no matter what type the object is, all the data values received from the function input() is String.

Therefore, to use the number from user as an Integer, we have to change it back to Integer like this example:

```
n = input("Enter a number: ")
doubleNum = int(n) * 2
print("The double of your number is ", doubleNum)
```

Output:

```
Debug I/O    Python Shell    Messages    OS Commands

Debug I/O (stdin, stdout, stderr) appears below

Enter a number: 5
The double of your number is   10
```

As we got the data value from the user through input() function, n equals "5". The statement int(n) did a great thing: changing a String "5" to an Integer 5 so that we can use it as an Integer later. Therefore, doubleNum equals 10 and it is printed out as a result.

📝 Check Your Understanding:

What is printed when the following code get executed? (Supposed the user types 2, then 3, and enter)

```
n = input("Enter a number: ")

m = input("Enter another number: ")

print(n + m)
```

Debug I/O   Python Shell   Messages   OS Commands

Debug I/O (stdin, stdout, stderr) appears below

Enter a number: 2
Enter a number: 3
 ???

A) 5

B) 3

C) 23

D) Error

✓ C is the correct answer because both n and m are Strings received from the user. That's why n + m equals "2" + "3", so the result is "23".

📝 Chapter Review Questions

1) Match the values on the left side with their appropriate types on the right side.

1) 9	A) String
2) "5"	B) Integer
3) 9.5	C) Float
4) False	D) Boolean

2) What is the output when the following code gets executed?

```
x = "tada"

x = 2.6

x = 7

print(x)
```

    A) tada
    B) 2.6
    C) 7
    D) Error

3) What is the output when the following code gets executed?

```
print((127//9)%5)
```

    A) 4
    B) 3
    C) 2
    D) 1

4) What is printed when the following code gets executed?

```
y = 8

y = y % 3

y = y ** 2
```

```
print( y == 4 )
```

A) 4

B) 16

C) True

D) False

5) Write a program to compute the area of a rectangle. Prompt the user to enter the width and height of the rectangle and print the answer back to show the user. For example if the user puts 4 and 6 for width and height, your program should print back 24 or 24.0 as the output.

6) Write a program that will convert degrees from the Celsius unit to the Fahrenheit unit. Prompt the users to enter the Celsius degree that they want to convert and give them back the answer. For example if the user puts 5, your program should print back 41 or 41.0 as the output.

(Hint: $T(°F) = T(°C) \times 1.8 + 32$)

7) Write a program that will convert degrees from the Fahrenheit unit to the Celsius unit. Prompt the users to enter the Fahrenheit degree that they want to convert and give them back the answer. For example if the user puts 41, your program should print back 5 or 5.0 as the output

(*) Check solutions on the next page after trying your best!

✓ **Solutions:**

1) 1-B, 2-A, 3-C, 4-D

2) C is the correct answer

3) A is the correct answer.

4) C is the correct answer.

5)

```
width = int(input("Enter the width of your regtangle: "))
height = int(input("Enter the height of your regtangle: "))
area = width * height
print(area)
```

6)

```
tempC = int(input("Type in temperature in Celsius degree: "))
tempF = tempC * 1.8 + 32
print(tempF)
```

7)

```
tempF = int(input("Type in temperature in Fahrenheit degree: "))
tempC = (tempF - 32) / 1.8
print(tempC)
```

CHAPTER 3: STRINGS

• Basics of Strings:

As mentioned before, Strings are anything covered by quotation marks.

For example:

"hello"

"abc123"

'tada'

"'%&#$^'"

" is called empty String. Empty String is covered by quotation marks but nothing inside the quotation marks.

Check the type of empty String:

```
print(type(''))
```

Output:

```
<class 'str'>
```

Yes. As you can see, even though there is nothing inside the quotation marks, it's still a String. It's called empty String.

• String & Operations:

The + operator represents not addition but **concatenation**, which means joining the two operands. For example:

```
a = "hello"
b = "world"
print(a+b)
```

Output:

```
helloworld
```

It can be seen that a + b means "hello" + "world", so the result will be the concatenation between these two strings. That's why we got "helloworld", which was joined by two parts of String.

It may be asked that why "helloworld" doesn't have blank space between two words and how we can have the blank space between "hello" and "world" in this case. This is the answer:

```
a = "hello"

b = "world"

print(a+ " "+ b)
```

Output:

```
hello world
```

Because + operator join Strings together, that's why we put the blank space between String a and String b. When all of these 3 things are joined, the blank space will appear between "hello" and "world" as a result.

The * operator performs repetition on strings. One of the operands must be a String and the other must be an Integer. For example:

```
print("a" * 3)

sound = "Hey"

print(sound * 3)
```

Output:

```
aaa
HeyHeyHey
```

"a" times 3 equals "aaa", which is 3 of "a" joined. In other words, "a" appeared 3 times. Similarly, "Hey" is repeated 3 times as the variable sound times 3, so we got "HeyHeyHey".

Let's take a look at another example to see how + operator and * operator work together:

```
print("Nope" + "!" * 3)
```

Output:

```
Nope!!!
```

First "!" will be repeated 3 times, so we got "!" * 3 equals "!!!". After that, "Nope" will combine with "!!!" to give the final output, which is "Nope!!!".

✍ Check Your Understanding:

1) What is printed when the following code executes?

```
first = "ne"
second = " ver"
print(first + second)
```

A) never
B) verne
C) ne ver
D) ver ne

2) What is printed when the following code executes?

```
st = "Yes"
print(st + "No" * 3)
print((st + "No") * 3)
```

A) YesNoNoNo
   YesYesYesNoNoNo

B) YesNoNoNo
   YesNoNoNo

C) YesNoNoNo
   YesNoYesNoYesNo

D) YesNoYesNoYesNo
   YesNoYesNoYesNo

✓ Answer:
1) C

When two variables first and second are added to each other, "ne" and " ver" are also joined. Be careful with the blank space in the variable second. If you take a look at the String " ver" carefully enough, you can see there is a little space in front. That's why "ne ver" is the output.

2) C

For the first line, the operator * has higher precedence so we have to calculate "No" * 3 first then evaluate the operate + later. "No" * 3 = "NoNoNo", and then "Yes" + "NoNoNo" equals YesNoNoNo. For the second line, the parentheses have the highest precedence, so "Yes" + "No" = "YesNo" is evaluated first. Then, "YesNo" * 3 equals "YesNoYesNoYesNo". Thus, C is the answer.

• String & Index:

The indexing operator, represented by brackets [ ], allows us to select one or many characters wanted from a string. The characters in a String are accessed and chosen by index values.

Remember that computer scientists often start counting from zero.

The index value starts from 0 and keeps counting up 1,2,3,... if you go from the left.

On the other hand, the index value starts from -1 and keeps going down to -2, -3, -4, ... if you go from the right side.

Let's take a look at the String "Hello World" for example:

0	1	2	3	4	5	6	7	8	9	10
H	e	l	l	o		W	o	r	l	d
-11	-10	-9	-8	-7	-6	-5	-4	-3	-2	-1

From image above, it can be seen that the letter "W" in the string has two index values: 6 and -5.

```
myString = "Hello World"
print(myString[4])
print(myString[-3])
```

Output:

```
o
r
```

Counting from the left to right, the expression myString[4] selects the character at index 4 from "Hello World", and creates "o". On the other hand, if the index value is a negative number, we count from the right and start at -1 instead of 0. So the character at index -3 is "r".

1) What is printed by the following statements?

```
name = "Michael Jackson"
print(name[4])
```

A) h
B) a
C) c
D) k

2) What is printed by the following statements?

```
name = "Michael Jackson"
print(name[4] + name[-6])
```

A) ha
B) aJ
C) aa
D) hJ

✓ Answer:

1) B

To find the index value in this question, we count from the left to right and start from 0 because 4 is a positive number. Therefore, the expression name[4] selects the character at index 4 from "Michael Jackson" and creates "a".

2) C

Similarly, name[4] is "a". When the index value is negative number, we count from right to left and start from -1. By this way, name[-6] equals "a". Joining two Strings, we have "a" + "a" = "aa". Thus, "aa" is the answer for this question.

• **Length of String:**

In Python, the len function applied to a String - len(aString) - returns the number of characters in that String.

For example:

```
name = "Alibaba"
print(len(name))
```

Output:

```
7
```

There are 7 characters in "Alibaba", so it returns 7.

Be careful. The last index of a String is not equal to the length of that String.

```
name = "Alibaba"
length = len(name)
lastItem = name[length]
print(lastItem)
```

Output:

```
builtins.IndexError: string index out of range.
```

There are 7 characters in this String, so the length must be 7. However, the last character of the String has the index value 6. This is because we start to count the first index from 0, not 1. Therefore, there is no index 7 in this String even though "Alibaba" has 7 characters.

This is how you can fix this:

```
name = "Alibaba"
length = len(name)
lastItem = name[length-1]
print(lastItem)
```

Output:

```
a
```

As mentioned above, the variable length is 7, so length – 1 equals 6. Therefore, lastItem at the index 6 is "a", which is output expected.

✎ Check Your Understanding:

What is printed by the following statements?

```
name = "Michael Jackson"
print(name[len(name)-6])
```

    A) a
    B) c
    C) J
    D) 9

✓ A is the correct answer. As we can evaluate, len(name) is 15 because there are 15 characters including white space in this String. So 15 – 6 = 9. At the index positon 9 of the String "Michael Jackson", the character is "a", which is the expected output.

• Slice Operator of String:

We learned how to get an item from a String by the given index. Now, let's see how we can get not only one but also many characters from a String. Slice operator will help us to do that.

```
say = "Welcome to the hotel California"

print(say[0:7])

print(say[15:20])

print(say[21:31])
```

Output:

```
Welcome
hotel
California
```

In the code, say[0:7] means it will take characters whose index is ranged from 0 upto 6 (it doesn't reach 7), so "Welcome" are characters which have index from 0 to 6. Similarly, "hotel" locates at index position from 15 to 19, and "California" locates at index position from 21 to 30.

How about if sometimes we don't know exactly where to start or where to end?

```
name = "alibaba"

print(name[:3])

print(name[3:])
```

Output:

```
ali
baba
```

On the code above, name[:3] means it will take all the characters from the String name from the beginning upto 2 (3 is not reached). On the other hand, name[3:] means all characters from index 3 to the end of the String will be collected. In other words, if we don't give the starting point in slice operator, Python will start at the beginning; if we don't know where to stop, Python will go to the end of the String. That's why "ali" and "baba" is printed out because "ali" have index position from zero upto 2, while "baba" locates from index positon 3 to the last index.

✎ Check Your Understanding:

What is printed by the following statements?

```
name = "Michael Jackson"
print(name[:7] * 3)
```

A) Michael Michael Michael
B) MichaelMichaelMichael
C) III
D) Jackson Jackson Jackson

✓ B is the correct answer. As name[:7] takes the characters at index position from 0 to 6, "Michael" is the collected. After that, "Michael" * 3 equals "MichaelMichaelMichael". Be careful with the blank space matter.

• Some Methods of String:

There are a lot of String methods built in Python. However, in this book, we just mention some of them, which are useful and suitable for those who start learning to code.

For more information, you can check the link below to discover more String methods built in Python:

https://docs.python.org/3/library/stdtypes.html#string-methods

Supposed we have a String called s. Here are some methods of String:

- **s.lower()** - Returns the lowercase version of the string.
- **s.upper()** - Returns the uppercase version of the string.
- **s.strip()** - Returns a string with whitespace removed.
- **s.isalpha()** - Returns True if all characters in the string are alphabetic or returns False if at least one character is not.
- **s.isdigit()** - Returns True if all characters in the string are decimal characters or returns False if there is at least one character that is not.
- **s.count(item)** - Returns the number of occurrences of item
- **s.startswith(item)** - Returns True if the string starts with the given item or returns False otherwise.
- **s.endswith(item)** - Returns True if the string ends with the given item or returns False otherwise.
- **s.find(item)** - Returns left most index if the item can be found in the String s or returns -1 if the item cannot be found.
- **s.replace (oldItem, newItem)** - Returns a String with all occurrences of old item have been replaced by new item.
- **s.split(string)** - Returns a List made by a String given (examples can show it more clearly).
- **s.join(list)** - opposite of split(), make a String by joining elements in the given list together (examples can show more).

Here are some examples of using String methods:

```
s = "Hello World"
print(s.lower())
print(s.upper())
```

Output:

```
hello world
HELLO WORLD
```

This is how we use lower() and upper() methods to make all the characters of the String become lowercase or uppercase.

Another example about String method:

```
s = "   Hello World   "
print(s + "!")
print(s.strip() + "!")
```

Output:

```
   Hello World   !
Hello World!
```

It can be seen that the white spaces in the original String make some blank spaces shown in the output. They are the blank space on the left of the letter "H" and the other blank space on the left of "!" in the first line of output. However, in the second line, all of these blank spaces are removed because of the strip() method.

The next example about String methods:

```
s1 = "abc def ghi"
s2 = "asdfgh"
print(s1.isalpha())
print(s2.isalpha())
s3 = "250609"
s4 = "2468!"
print(s3.isdigit())
print(s4.isdigit())
```

Output:

```
False
True
True
False
```

It looks like there are just alphabetic characters in the String s1 because there is not any number or symbol contained in s1. However, the blank space in String s1 is not alphabetic character. Therefore, it makes "abc def ghi" is not a String containing just alphabetic characters. That's why s1.isalpha() is False, while s2.isalpha() is True. Similarly, unlike s3 which contains just numbers, s4 also has "!" at the end of the String. That's why s4.isdigit() is False.

Let's take a look at count(item) method:

```
s = "alibaba"
print(s.count("a"))
```

Output:

```
3
```

There are 3 letters "a" in the String "alibaba", so the output is 3.

Example of startswith() and endswith() method:

```
s = "Hannah"

print(s.startswith("h"))

print(s.endswith("h"))
```

Output:

```
False
True
```

The String s starts with letter "H", not "h". That's why s.startswith("h") is False. String is case-sensitive, so be careful. On the other hand, s.endswith("h") is True because "h" is the last character in the String s.

Example of find() method:

```
s = "Michael Jackson"

print(s.find("a"))

print(s.find("y"))
```

Output:

```
4
-1
```

There are two letters "a" in the String s: one locates at the index 4, and the other one locates at the index 9. The one has the index of 4 is the leftmost, so it returns

4 at the first line. On the other hand, "y" is not in the String "Michael Jackson", so it returns -1 as we mentioned before.

Here is the example about replace(oldItem, newItem) method:

```
s = "alibaba"
print(s.replace("a","o"))
```

Output:

```
olibobo
```

The method helps to replace all the chosen old characters by the chosen new characters. In this case, all letters "a" in "alibaba" change to "o", making the String s become "olibobo".

Finally, the split() and join() methods that we mentioned before requires some understanding of Python lists. Therefore, we will talk more about them at the next chapter: Lists.

✎ Check Your Understanding:

1) What is printed by the following statements?

```
say = "welcome to the hotel California"
print(say.count("o") + say.count("e"))
```

A) "oe"
B) 8
C) 9
D) Error

2) What is printed by the following statements?

```
say = "welcome to the hotel California"
print(say[-3] * say.find("o"))
```

A) nnnn
B) ooo
C) 3
D) Error

✓ Answer:
1) B

There are 4 letters "o" and 4 letters "e" in the String "welcome to the hotel California". Therefore, say.count("o") returns 4, and say.count("e") also returns 4. After that, 4 + 4 = 8, which is the output of the code.

2) A

First of all, at the index -3 of the String "welcome to the hotel California", the value of the item is "n". Besides, say.find("o") returns 4 because the left-most index of letter "o" in this String is 4. Finally, "n" * 4 = "nnnn", which is the answer of this question.

• String Comparison:

Strings are comparable by operators which are like relational operators such as ==, != , > , >= , < , and <= . The String comparison is similar to the alphabetical order rule used in a dictionary. The word coming before is less than the word coming after. In addition, all the uppercase letters come before all the lowercase letters.

For example:

```
a = "alibaba"

b = "simba"

print(a == "alibaba")

print(a == b)
```

Output:

```
True
False
```

It can be seen that "alibaba" is "alibaba" and every letter in String a matches with every letter in "alibaba", so a == "alibaba" is True. By contrast, "simba" is not "alibaba", so a == b is False.

Example of comparisons based on alphabetical order rule:

```
print("apple" > "google")

print("microsoft" < "yahoo")

print("Ibm" == "ibm")

print("Oracle" < "oracle")
```

Output:

```
False
True
False
True
```

As letter "a" comes before letter "g" in alphabet, "apple" should be before "google" in dictionary. Therefore, "apple" > "google" is False. Similarly, "microsoft" come before "yahoo", so "microsoft" < "yahoo". "Ibm" and "ibm" are not the same because "I" is different from "i". Finally, as capitalized letters come before lower-case letters, "Oracle" is less than "oracle", so "Oracle" < "oracle" is True.

✎ Check Your Understanding:

What is printed by the following statements?

```
print("Big" < "Bigbang")
print("Big" < "big")
print("big" < "Bigbang")
```

A) True
   True
   False

B) True
   False
   False

C) False
   True
   False

D) False
   False
   True

✓ Answer: A is the correct answer. In the first line, both Strings match 3 first letters but "Big" is shorter than "Bigbang" so it comes before the other in the dictionary. In the second line, upper case is less than lower case as we mentioned before. Finally, lower case "b" is greater than upper case "B" even though "big" is shorter than "Bigbang". Therefore, "big" < "Bigbang" is False.

• Immutable String:

In Python, String is immutable. In other words, Python does not allow you to modify characters in the String.

Example:

```
word = "Ball"
word[0] = "T"
print(word)
```

Output:

```
builtins.TypeError: 'str' object does not support item assignment
```

As we learned before, the "=" sign is for assigning value to variable. It seems the code wants to change the word "Ball" to "Tall" by trying to make the letter "B" become "T". However, String is immutable, and we cannot change any character in a given String.

This is how we can change the old word from "Ball" to "Tall"

```
word = "Ball"
print(word)
newWord = "T" + word[1:]
print(newWord)
```

Output:

```
Ball
Tall
```

As we learned before, word[1:] represents the String from index 1 to the end of that String, which is "all" in this case. Therefore, "T" + "all" = "Tall" based on concatenation rule mentioned before in String.

• in or not in String:

In Python, the **in** operator checks if a String is inside another String or not. On the other hand, the **not in** operator checks if a String is **not** inside another String or not.

For example:

```
print("h" in "hello")
print("a" in "hello")
print("" in "hello")
print("he" in "hello")
print("eh" in "hello")
```

Output:

```
True
False
True
True
False
```

There is a letter "h" in "hello", so it's True that "h" in "hello". By contrast, "a" does not show up in "hello", so "a" in "hello" is False. An empty String is in "hello" as any String can contain empty String. Additionally, "he" is a part of "hello", so "he" is in "hello". However, "eh" is not in "hello" because it's not a part of "hello although two single letter "e" and "h" are both in "hello".

Examples about **not in** operator:

```
print("h" not in "hello")
print("a" not in "hello")
print("" not in "hello")
print("he" not in "hello")
print("eh" not in "hello")
```

Output:

```
False
True
False
False
True
```

As we can see, the output is completely opposite to the output of the previous example. It's simply that **not in** is opposite to **in**. It's True that "h" is **in** "hello", but it's False that "h" is **not in** "hello". We can apply the same rule to the rest.

✎ Chapter Review Questions:

1) What is printed when the code below gets executed?

```
print("a"+" b"+"c "+"d")
```

    A) abcd
    B) a b c d
    C) abc d
    D) a bc d

2) What is printed when the code below gets executed?

```
name = "Luther College"
print(name[3] + name[-4])
```

    A) hl
    B) tl
    C) he
    D) -1

3) What is printed by the following statements below?

```
name = "Luther College"
print(name[len(name)-3])
```

    A) e
    B) l
    C) t
    D) h

4) What is printed by the following statements below?

```
name = "Luther College"
print(name[:2] * 3)
```

A) LutLutLut

B) LuLuLu

C) Lut Lut Lut

D) Lu Lu Lu

5) Strings are immutable. True or False?

6)

```
s = "This is a String"
print(s[-3] * s.count("s"))
```

A) sss

B) iii

C) ii

D) rrr

(*) Check solutions on the next page after trying your best!

✓ Solutions:

1) D

2) A

3) A

4) B

5) True

6) C

CHAPTER 4: LISTS

• What is Python List?

A Python list is a collection of data values, which are identified and collected by index. Similar to strings, lists are built by collections of elements inside the list. However, elements of a list can have any type. In other words, elements can be different types.

This is how lists look like in Python:

[1,2,3,4,5]

["a", "b", "c", "d"]

[1, "a", 5, "f"]

It is noted that a list can be inside another list. For example:

["h", "s", 4, 6, [2, "b", "f", 6], "t", 7]

There are ways to declare a new list. One of the ways we recommend is using brackets [ ] to enclose items. For example:

```
words = ["q", "w", "e", "r", "t"]

numbers = [6, 25, 9]

mixedList = [words,numbers]

print(words)

print(numbers)

print(mixedList)
```

Output:

```
['q', 'w', 'e', 'r', 't']

[6, 25, 9]

[['q', 'w', 'e', 'r', 't'], [6, 25, 9]]
```

The code above showed how to declare Python lists and how they are printed.

• Length of List:

The length of Python list is the number of elements inside the list, which can be evaluated by the len function expressed as len(alist). It is noted that a list can be an element inside another list, so it's counted as one element of that list. For example:

```
list1 = ["a",2,9,"t"]

list2 = [2,6,["a","b"],8,5,[1,2,"f"]]

print(len(list1))

print(len(list2))
```

Output:

```
4
6
```

It is clear that the list1 has 4 elements which are "a", 2, 9, and "t". On the other hand, it's more tricky to see the actual length of list2. We can see 2, 6, "a", "b", 8, 5, 1, 2, and "f" inside the list2. However, "a" and "b" are in another small list inside, and 1,2, and "f" are also in small list inside. These small lists are just elements of list2. Therefore, ["a", "b"] or [1, 2, "f"] is counted as 1 element is the list2. That's why list1 has 4 elements, while list2 has 6 elements instead of 9.

✎ Check Your Understanding:

What is printed by the following statements?

```
myList = [1,2,[3,4,5],6,[7,8,[9,10]],11,12]

print(len(myList))
```

A) 7

B) 8

C) 9

D) 12

A is the correct answer. The list is mixed by many smaller lists inside, so it is difficult to see the actual length of this list. This list contains 7 elements: 1, 2, the list [3,4,5], 6, 7, the complicated list [7,8,[9,10]], 11 and 12.

• List & Index:

Similar to String, List also has the index operator which is represented by brackets [ ]. It allows us to access and select one or many characters wanted from a List. The characters in a List are accessed and chosen by index values.

Similar to String, List's index starts from zero.

The index value starts from 0 and keeps counting up 1,2,3,... if you go from the left.

On the other hand, the index value starts from -1 and keeps going down to -2, -3, -4, ... if you go from the right side.

Let's take a look at the following example:

```
mylist = ["q","w","e","r","t","y"]
print(mylist[1])
print(mylist[-2])
print(mylist[7-5])
print(mylist[len(mylist) - 3])
```

Output:

```
w

t

e

r
```

As the index of the List starts at 0, mylist[1] returns "w", the elements locates at the index position 1. Besides, -2 is a negative number, so we count from the right to left and start at -1. That's why mylist[-2] returns "t". Next, mylist[7-5] means mylist[2], and the element at the index location 2 is "e". Finally, len(mylist) is 6, so mylist[len(mylist)-3]) is mylist[3], which is "r".

Next, how can we access elements which are inside another smaller lists inside the list given? This is how we solve this problem:

```
myList = [1,2,[3,4,5],6,[7,8,[9,10]],11,12]
print(myList[2][1])
```

Output:

```
4
```

The statement myList[2][1] means first we go to the element at the index positon 2 of myList, which is the small list [3,4,5]. After that, we go to the element at the index position 1 of the element we just accessed before. In this case, 4 is the element at the index position 1 of [3,4,5]. Thus, 4 is printed out.

 Check Your Understanding:

What is printed by the following statements?

```
myList = [1,2,[3,4,5],6,[7,8,[9,10]],11,12]
print(myList[4][2][1])
```

A) 9

B) 10

C) 8

D) IndexError: list index out of range on line 2

✓ Answer:

B is the correct answer. First, myList[4] is [7,8,[9,10]]. After that, myList[4][2] will access the element at the index position 2 of the list [7,8,[9,10]], so it is [9,10]. Finally, myList[4][2][1] will take the element at the position 1 of the list [9,10], which is 10. Hence, 10 is the output.

• List & Slices:

We learned how to get an item from a List by the given index. Now, let's see how we can get not only one but also many elements from a given List. Slice operator will help us to do that.

```
myList = ["q", "w", "e", "r", "t", "y"]
print(myList[1:4])
print(myList[:3])
print(myList[3:])
print(myList[:])
```

Output:

```
['w', 'e', 'r']
['q', 'w', 'e']
['r', 't', 'y']
['q', 'w', 'e', 'r', 't', 'y']
```

In the code, myList[1:4] means it will take elements whose index is ranged from 1 upto 4 (4 is not included), so 'w', 'e', 'r' are elements which have index from 1 to 3.

Next, myList[:3] means it will take all the elements from myList from the beginning upto 2 (3 is not reached). On the other hand, myList[3:] means all elements from index 3 to the end of myList will be accessed. In other words, if we don't give the starting point in slice operator, Python will start at the beginning; if we don't know where to stop, Python will go to the end of the List. That's why ['q', 'w', 'e'] is printed out because this List contains items which have index position from zero upto 2. Similarly, ['r', 't', 'y'] is printed out because this List contains items which have index position from 2 to the end of myList.

Finally, myList[:] means it starts at the beginning and goes to the end of myList, so all elements in myList are printed out.

🐾 Check Your Understanding:

What is printed by the following statements?

```
myList = [1,2,[3,4,5],6,[7,8,[9,10]],11,12]
print(myList[3:])
```

A) [6, [7, 8, [9, 10]], 11, 12]
B) [[7, 8, [9, 10]], 11, 12]
C) [[9, 10], 11, 12]
D) [1,2,[3,4,5]]

✓ Answer:

A is the correct answer. In the code, myList[3:] takes elements from index 3 to the end of the list. 6 is the element at index 3, and 12 is the element at the end of myList. Therefore, [6, [7, 8, [9, 10]], 11, 12] is printed out.

• List & Operators:

Working as they do with String, the + operator concatenates lists, and the * operator repeats the items in a list.

For example

```
words = ["a","b","c","d"]
numbers = [1,2,3,4]
print(words + numbers)
print(words * 3)
print(words * 2 + numbers * 2)
```

Output:

```
['a', 'b', 'c', 'd', 1, 2, 3, 4]
['a', 'b', 'c', 'd', 'a', 'b', 'c', 'd', 'a', 'b', 'c', 'd']
['a', 'b', 'c', 'd', 'a', 'b', 'c', 'd', 1, 2, 3, 4, 1, 2, 3, 4]
```

It can be seen that all elements in list words and list numbers are concatenated and brought together into one new list. On the other hand, all of elements in list words are repeated three times as words * 3. Finally, the last line of the output is the double of list words concatenated with the double of list numbers.

🖎 Check Your Understanding:

1) What is printed by the following statements?

```
odds = [1, 3, 5]
evens = [2, 4, 6]
print(odds + evens)
```

A) [1, 3, 5, 2, 4, 6]
B) [1, 2, 3, 4, 5, 6]
C) oddsevens
D) [3, 7, 11]

2) What is printed by the following statements?

```
myList = [1, 2, 3]

print(myList * 3)
```

A) [3, 6, 9]
B) [3, 6, 9, 3, 6, 9, 3, 6, 9]
C) [1, 2, 3, 1, 2, 3, 1, 2, 3]
D) [1, 1, 1, 2, 2, 2, 3, 3, 3]

✓ Answer:
1) A

The ouput is supposed to show a new list with all elements of the first list followed by all elements from the second list. Thus, the new list should be [1, 3, 5, 2, 4, 6], which is also printed as output.

2) C

All items of myList are supposed to be repeated 3 times in the code above. Therefore, [1, 2, 3, 1, 2, 3, 1, 2, 3] is the output.

• List & Items:

First of all, **in** and **not in** are boolean operators to check if elements in a list of not. The way they work in List is very similar to the way they work in String that we learned before.

For example:

```
teams = ["roma", "milan", "liverpool", "chelsea"]
print("roma" in teams)
print("barcelona" in teams)
```

Output:

```
True
False
```

It can be seen that "roma" is an element of the list teams. Therefore, "roma" in teams is True. On the other hand, "barcelona" is not an element of the list, so "barcelona" in teams is False.

Another example about **not in:**

```
numbers = [1,1,2,3,5,8,13,21,34]
print(8 not in numbers)
print(9 not in numbers)
```

Output:

```
False
True
```

It can be seen that 8 is a number inside the list numbers declared above. Therefore, saying 8 not in numbers is totally False. On the other hand, 9 not in numbers is True.

✓ Check Your Understanding:

What is printed by the following statements?

```
numbers = [1,2,[3,4,5],6,[7,[8,9],10],11,12]

print(7 not in numbers)
```

A) True
B) False

✓ A is the correct answer. It is kind of tricky when you see number 7 in the list
   numbers, but it is actually not in the list. 7 is just an element of a smaller list
   inside the list numbers, so it's not an element of the list numbers.
   Therefore, 7 not in numbers is True.

In addition, items in a List can be replaced as Lists, unlike Strings, are mutable.
Lists allow us to change an item in a list by accessing it.

```
names = ["Gus", "Grant", "Michael", "Isaiah", "Ales"]

print(names)

names[1] = "Blaise"

names[-1] = "Kirby"

print(names)
```

Output:

```
['Gus', 'Grant', 'Michael', 'Isaiah', 'Ales']
['Gus', 'Blaise', 'Michael', 'Isaiah', 'Kirby']
```

The first line of output prints exactly the original list names. After that, we
assigned new values to replace old values from the original list. "Grant" and
"Ales" were already replaced by "Blaise" and "Kirby", so the updated list now is
['Gus', 'Blaise', 'Michael', 'Isaiah', 'Kirby'].

In addition, it is noted that we can update a list by not only one element but also several elements by using slice operator. For example:

```
numbers = [1,3,5,7,9,11,13]

numbers[1:4] = [2,4]

print(numbers)
```

Output:

```
[1, 2, 4, 9, 11, 13]
```

Using the slice operator [1:4], we accessed elements of the list numbers from the index 1 to the index 3 (4 is not included). All elements in this range, which are 3, 5, and 7, are replaced by new numbers. Therefore, 2 and 4, new numbers supposed to replace 3, 5, and 7, now stay in the new list. The list numbers now becomes [1, 2, 4, 9, 11, 13].

Replacing elements inside a list sometimes is tricky, so be careful with every detail in your code. For example:

```
list1 = ['a', 'd', 'f', 'g']

list1[1:1] = ['b', 'c']

print(list1)

list2 = ['a', 'd', 'f', 'g']

list2[1] = ['b', 'c']

print(list2)
```

Output:

```
['a', 'b', 'c', 'd', 'f', 'g']

['a', ['b', 'c'], 'f', 'g']
```

74

In this situation, we created two identical lists called list1 and list2, which both are ['a', 'd', 'f', 'g']. However, the way we update these two lists are slightly different. Updating the list1, we try to put 'b' and 'c' inside the list1 at the index position 1 by using slice operator [1:1]. In this case, [1:1] means we start at the index 1 and go to the index 1 but not included 1, so 'd' is not removed from the list as it was in the index positon 1 of the old list and it is not included. Therefore, 'b' and 'c' are placed at the index position 1 without removing 'd'.

On the other hand, we update list2 without using slice operator. The statement list2[1] means we put the new element exactly at the index position 1, and the element at that position in the old list will be replaced. Therefore, 'd' was removed and replaced by ['b', 'c']. It is noted that, instead of 'b' and 'c', the small list ['b', 'c'] was placed in the new list. This makes sense because if 'b' and 'c' are put in, that means we put 2 elements inside the list while the list is supposed to receive just 1 element. Thus, ['b', 'c'] becomes the new element and 'd' is removed in this case.

How about if we replace old elements by an empty list?

```
numbers = ["q","w","e","r","t","y"]

numbers[1:4] = []

print(numbers)
```

Output:

```
['q', 't', 'y']
```

The code shows us that all the elements from index position 1 to 3 (4 is not included) are replaced by nothing as empty list contains nothing inside. That means "w", "e", and "r" are removed.

🖎 Check Your Understanding:

What is printed by the following statements?

```
myList = ["q","w","e","r","t","y","u","i","o","p"]
myList[-3] = "z"
myList[1:3] = ["a","s","d"]
myList[4:7] = []
print(myList)
```

A) ['q', 'a', 's', 'd', 'u', 'i', 'o', 'p']
B) ['q', 'w', 'e', 'r', 'z', 'o', 'p']
C) ['q', 'a', 's', 'd', 'r', 't', 'y', 'u', 'z', 'o', 'p']
D) ['q', 'a', 's', 'd', 'u', 'z', 'o', 'p']

✓ D is the correct answer. First, the element at the index position -3 is replaced by "z", so the list becomes ['q', 'w', 'e', 'r', 't', 'y', 'u', 'z', 'o', 'p']. After that, elements from index 1 to 2 (3 not included) are replaced by "a", "s", and "d". Now myList becomes ['q', 'a', 's', 'd', 'r', 't', 'y', 'u', 'z', 'o', 'p']. Finally, all elements from index position 4 to index position 6 (7 not included) are removed as we replace them by empty list, so myList now is ['q', 'a', 's', 'd', 'u', 'z', 'o', 'p'].

As we learned, elements in the list can be removed by simply replacing them by an empty list. However, many programmers are not really comfortable with slice operators. There is also another way to remove an element from a list. It is called **del**. The **del** keyword allows us to remove an element from a list by using its index position. For example:

o Delete one element:

```
numbers = [1,2,3,4,5]
del numbers[1]
print(numbers)
```

Output:

```
[1, 3, 4, 5]
```

It can be seen that the item at index position 1 was removed from the list.

o   Delete several elements:

```
chars = ["q","w","e","r","t","y"]
del chars[1:4]
print(chars)
```

Output:

```
['q', 't', 'y']
```

All the items from index position 1 to index position 3 (4 not included) were removed from the list.

• Reference & Alias of Lists:

Reference is a key factor in programming, and it is very confusing sometimes. First of all, let's see if we declare two Strings with the same value, do they refer to the same object.

```
stringA = "apple"
stringB = "apple"
print(stringA is stringB)
```

Output:

True

The output is True. That's mean stringA is string. In other words, they refer to the same object. The picture below describes this:

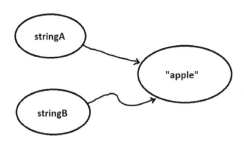

However, it is noted that String is immutable. Lists, on the other hand, are not immutable. Will two lists refer to the same object if we declare them with the same value?

```
listA = [1,2,3]
listB = [1,2,3]
print(listA is listB)
print(listA == listB)
```

Output:

```
False
True
```

In this case, listA is not listB even though they are declared exactly with the same values. They can be equal (==) as they have the same values, but they cannot be each other as they refer to different objects. The graph below explains this.

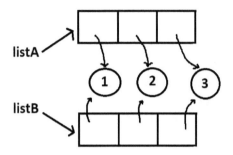

It is still False to say listA is listB even though we created listB exactly by the same way and elements we created listA. So the question here is how we can make both variables refer to the same object?

```
listA = [1, 2, 3]
listB = listA
print(listB)
print(listA is listB)
```

Output:

```
[1, 2, 3]
True
```

Different from the previous example, listB now refers to the same object as listA does. This is because the way we declared listB is different. Last time, we declared listB by assigning listB to the same values as listA assigned to. However, now we assign listB directly to listA by saying listB = listA. Therefore, now the statement listA is listB is True. The diagram below can demonstrate clearly this situation:

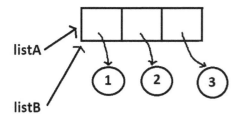

The picture shows that the same list has two different names: listA and listB. This is called alias. It can be seen that listA and listB refer to the same list (the rectangle with 3 spots portrayed) because of the statement listB = listA.

✌ Quick Question:

What is printed by the following statements?

listA = [1,2,3,4,5,6]
listB = listA
listB[2] = 30
print(listA)

A) [1,2,3,4,5,6]
B) [1,2,30,4,5,6]

B is the correct answer. From the code above, it looks like we just changed one element in listB without touching listA. However, the element in listA also changes when the element in listB changes because both of them actually refers to the same object. In other words, listA is listB, so if one of them change, the other one will also change the same way.

So how about if we want to make another list look like the original list, but the original list is too long and too complicated to redo it again. Additionally, we also don't want these two lists refer to the same object because when we make some changes in one list, the other one will be affected. What can we do?

This is the answer:

```
listA = [1,2,3,4,5,6]
listB = listA[:]
print(listB)
listA[2] = 300
print(listA)
print(listB)
```

Output:

```
[1, 2, 3, 4, 5, 6]
[1, 2, 300, 4, 5, 6]
[1, 2, 3, 4, 5, 6]
```

This process is called cloning, which helps us to modify a copied list and keep the original unchanged. The slice operator [:] clones the list by consisting elements from the beginning to the end of the original list.

🖐 Challenge:

What is printed by the following statements?

```
listA = [1,2,3,4,5]
listB = [listA] * 3
listA[2] = 123
print(listB)
```

A) [1, 2, 3, 4, 5]
B) [[1, 2, 123, 4, 5], [1, 2, 3, 4, 5], [1, 2, 3, 4, 5]]
C) [1, 2, 3, 4, 5, 1, 2, 3, 4, 5, 1, 2, 3, 4, 5]
D) [[1, 2, 123, 4, 5], [1, 2, 123, 4, 5], [1, 2, 123, 4, 5]]

✓ D is the correct answer. In the code, listB = [listA] * 3, so listB becomes [[1, 2, 3, 4, 5], [1, 2, 3, 4, 5], [1, 2, 3, 4, 5]], not [1, 2, 3, 4, 5, 1, 2, 3, 4, 5, 1, 2, 3, 4, 5] because of the brackets covered listA. Furthermore, it can be seen that listA was part of listB when listB was declared, so when we make some changes in listA, listB also changes. Therefore, the updated listB shows changes in three places as listA was repeated 3 times in listB.

• Some Methods of Lists:

There are a lot of List methods built in Python. However, in this section, we just mention some of them, which I believe useful and suitable for students who start to learn how to code.

For more information, you can check the link below to discover more List methods built in Python:

https://docs.python.org/3/tutorial/datastructures.html

Declaring a Lists call mylist, we have some methods of Lists:

- **mylist.append(item)** - adds a new single element to the end of the list.
- **mylist.insert(index, item)** - inserts the new element at the given index.
- **mylist.index(item)** - returns the index position of first occurrence of the item.
- **mylist.remove(item)** - remove the first instance of the given item.
- **mylist.sort()** - sorts the list but does not return it.
- **mylist.reverse()** - reverses the list in order but does not return it.
- **mylist.pop(index)** - removes and returns the element at the given index.

Here are some examples of using List methods:

```
mylist = []
mylist.append(6)
mylist.append(25)
mylist.append(200)
mylist.append(9)
print(mylist)


mylist.insert(2,14)
print(mylist)
```

Output:

```
[6, 25, 200, 9]
[6, 25, 14, 200, 9]
```

The variable mylist started as an empty list. After that, the append method added 6, 25, 200, and 9 to the end of the list in order. That's why [6, 25, 200, 9] was printed out. On the other hand, the insert method allows us to put an item at any position in the list, so number 14 was placed at the index position 2 as expected.

Example about mylist.index(item):

```
mylist = [6,25,14,200,9]
print(mylist.index(14))
```

Output:

```
2
```

The code returns the index position of the item 14, so 2 is printed.

Example about remove and pop methods:

```
mylist = [1,1,2,3,5,8,13,21,34,55]
print(mylist.remove(13))
print(mylist)
print(mylist.pop(4))
print(mylist)
```

Output:

```
None
[1, 1, 2, 3, 5, 8, 21, 34, 55]
5
[1, 1, 2, 3, 8, 21, 34, 55]
```

Both remove and pop methods deleted items inside the list. The difference between the remove and pop methods is that we give the remove method the item to be removed, while we give the pop method the position of the item we want to remove. Furthermore, the remove method doesn't return anything, but the pop method returns the item at the position we want to remove.

Example about sort and reverse of a List:

```
listA = [5,8,2,3,4,7,1]
listB = [5,7,2,4,3,8,9]
listA.reverse()
listB.sort()
print(listA)
print(listB)
```

Output:

```
[1, 7, 4, 3, 2, 8, 5]
[2, 3, 4, 5, 7, 8, 9]
```

It can be seen from the output that listA was already reversed by the statement listA.reverse() and listB was already sorted from smallest to biggest numbers. It is also noted that if we write print(listB.sort()) or print(listA.reverese()), we will not see any result turn in as we expect because these two methods just modify the lists instead of returning the lists after updating.

✎ Check Your Understanding:

What is printed by the following statements?

```
mylist = [5,8,2,3,4,7,1]

mylist.append(6)

mylist.append(9)

mylist.remove(8)

mylist.pop(3)

mylist.insert(3,8)

print(mylist)
```

A) [5, 2, 3, 8, 7, 1, 6, 9]
B) [5, 8, 2, 3, 4, 7, 1]
C) [5, 8, 2, 3, 7, 1, 6, 9]
D) [5, 2, 3, 7, 1, 6, 9, 8]

✓ A is the correct answer. 6 and 9 are put at the tail of the list, while 8 and 4 (which is at index 3 after 8 was removed) were taken out of the list. 8 was put back to the list at the position 3 after that.

• The relation between Strings and Lists:

Remember when I said in the previous chapter: "the split() and join() methods requires some understanding of Python lists. Therefore, we will talk more about them at the next chapter: Lists."

Now, this is the time.

First, the **split** method breaks a string into a list of elements. By default, the whitespace separates every single element collected to the list, but we can modify the word boundaries. For example:

o Splitting by default:

```
aString = "this is an example you need to know."

aList = aString.split()

print(aList)
```

Output:

```
['this', 'is', 'an', 'example', 'you', 'need', 'to', 'know.']
```

All words in aString are broken into every single item in aList. It is noted that all these are separated by whitespace in aString, so by default the split() method understands that every word is an item of aList and whitespaces are word boundaries.

o Splitting by a specified word boundary:

```
aString = "a@b@c@d e@f@g @h@i" #notice 2 whitespaces

listA = aString.split()

listB = aString.split("@")

print(listA)

print(listB)
```

Output:

```
['a@b@c@d', 'e@f@g', '@h@i']

['a', 'b', 'c', 'd e', 'f', 'g ', 'h', 'i']
```

It can be seen that listA is made by elements broken by default from aString, while listB is made by items broken by "@" as word boundary. As a result, elements in listA are 3 parts separated by whitespaces: "a@b@c@d", "e@f@g", and "@h@i". On the other hand, listB has 8 items split by 7 "@" symbols in aString: 'a', 'b', 'c', 'd e', 'f', 'g ', 'h', and 'i'.

Two examples above are about how to make a String become a List. How about making a List become a String?

```
mylist = ["a","b","c","d","e"]

print(" ".join(mylist))

print("".join(mylist))

print("-".join(mylist))
```

Output:

```
a b c d e

abcde

a-b-c-d-e
```

It can be seen that the join() method connected items in mylist into a String. In the first printing line, " ", which is the whitespace inside the quotation marks, make elements separated by whitespaces in the new String. Besides, in the second printing line, an empty String "" is chosen to glue elements in mylist. That's why nothing separates them in the newString, making the newString appear as "abcde". Finally, "-" is the last glue in this example, so all elements are connected by "-" in the new String as we expected.

What is printed by the following statements?

```
a = "a_b_c_d_e_f_g"

b = a.split("_")

c = b[:3]

d = " ".join(c)

print(d)
```

A) abc
B) a b c
C) abcdefg
D) a b c d e f g

✓ B is the correct answer. First of all, the variable a is split into a List, which is variable b, so b is ['a', 'b', 'c', 'd', 'e', 'f', 'g']. After that, c takes elements of b from index position 0 up to 2 (3 is not include), so c becomes ['a', 'b', 'c']. Finally, d is a String made by elements 'a', 'b', and 'c' which all are glued by whitespaces. Thus, the output is "a b c" as expected.

In addition to split method, there is another way to make a String turn into a List:

```
aString = "how are you doing?"

listA = aString.split()

listB = list(aString)

print(listA)

print(listB)
```

Output:

```
['how', 'are', 'you', 'doing?']

['h', 'o', 'w', ' ', 'a', 'r', 'e', ' ', 'y', 'o', 'u', ' ', 'd', 'o', 'i', 'n', 'g', '?']
```

It can be clearly seen that both listA and listB are made from aString. However, while listA contains words in aString, list B contains every single characters including whitespaces in aString. Therefore, split() method breaks aString into elements separated by whitespaces, but the other technique list(aString) breaks aString into every single characters and doesn't care about word boundaries.

🖎 Chapter Review Questions:

1) What is printed by the following statements?

```
myList = [1,[2,3,4],5,6,[7,8,[9,10],11],12]

print(len(myList))
```

    A) 6
    B) 7
    C) 8
    D) 12

2) What is printed by the following statements?

```
myList = [1,[2,3,4],5,6,[7,8,[9,10],11],12]

print(myList[4][2])
```

    A) 8
    B) 9
    C) 10
    D) [9,10]

3) What is printed by the following statements?

```
myList = [1,[2,3,4],5,6,[7,8,[9,10],11],12]

print(myList[3:5])
```

    A) [4, 5]
    B) [6, [7, 8, [9, 10], 11]]
    C) [6, [7, 8, [9, 10], 11], 12]
    D) [7, 8, [9, 10]]

4) What is printed by the following statements?

```
a = [1,2]
b = [3,4]
print(a*2+b)
```

    A) [2, 4, 3, 4]
    B) [5, 8]
    C) [[1, 2], [1, 2], [3, 4]]
    D) [1, 2, 1, 2, 3, 4]

5) What is printed by the following statements?

```
myList = [1,[2,3,4],5,6,[7,8,[9,10],11],12]
print(8 in myList)
```

    A) True
    B) False

6) What is printed by the following statements?

```
myList = ["a","b","c","d","e","f","g","h","i","j"]
myList[-3] = "x"
myList[1:3] = ["l","m","n","o"]
myList[4:7] = []
print(myList)
```

    A) ['a', 'b', 'c', 'd', 'x', 'i', 'j']
    B) ['a', 'l', 'm', 'n', 'f', 'g', 'x', 'i', 'j']
    C) ['a', 'l', 'm', 'n', 'g', 'x', 'i', 'j']
    D) ['a', 'l', 'm', 'n', 'o', 'd', 'e', 'f', 'g', 'x', 'i', 'j']

7) What is printed by the following statements?

```
listA = [1,2,3]

listB = [listA] * 3

listA[1] = 7

print(listB)
```

A) [1, 2, 3]
B) [[1, 7, 3], [1, 2, 3], [1, 2, 3]]
C) [[1, 7, 3], [1, 7, 3], [1, 7, 3]]
D) [1, 7, 3, 1, 7, 3, 1, 7, 3]

8) What is printed by the following statements?

```
a = "a b c d e f"

b = a.split()

c = b[:3]

d = "-".join(c)

print(d)
```

A) a-b-c
B) a-b-c-d
C) a b c
D) abc

(*) Check solutions on the next page after trying your best!

✓ **Solutions**

1) A

2) D

3) B

4) D

5) B

6) B

7) C

8) A

CHAPTER 5: TUPLE & DICTIONARY

• What is Tuple?

Tuple is something between List and String. To be more detailed, like a list, tuple is a collection of items of any type, and all the items of a tuple are covered by parentheses (). However, tuple is immutable. Remember that strings are immutable and lists are mutable.

This is how tuples look like in Python:

(1, 2, 3, 4)

("a", 2, "b", 7, "c")

Tuples have a lot of characteristics similar to Lists. The ways of declaration, using slice operators, len function, and other stuffs work in Tuples is very similar to the ways they work in Lists. For example:

```
aTuple = ("ronaldo", 7, "batigol", 9, "totti", 10, "gerrard", 8, "reus", 11)

print(len(aTuple))

print(aTuple[6])

print(aTuple[2:6])
```

Output:

```
10
gerrard
('batigol', 9, 'totti', 10)
```

The first line of output shows how many elements in aTuple, and the second line shows the item at the index position 6 of aTuple, which is "gerrard". Finally, using slice operator [2:6] takes the items at index position from 2 to 5 (6 is not included), so 'batigol', 9, 'totti', and 10 are collected.

Noticeably, if we want to create a tuple containing just only one single element, we have to include the final comma. For example:

```
a = (4,)
print(type(a))
b = (4)
print(type(b))
```

Output:

```
<class 'tuple'>
<class 'int'>
```

As you can see, if we don't use final comma in the tuple, Python understands (4) is an integer, not a tuple.

• Immutable Tuple:

Like Strings, Tuples are immutable. That means we cannot change or modify items inside a Tuple declared.

```
aTuple = ("ronaldo", 7, "batigol", 9, "totti", 10, "gerrard", 8, "reus", 11)
aTuple[4] = "zidane"
print(aTuple)
```

Output:

```
builtins.TypeError: 'tuple' object does not support item assignment
```

As you can see in the code, we are trying to replace "totti" by "zidane". However, Tuples are immutable so we cannot do that.

• Efficient Tuple Assignment:

In Python, using Tuple assignment is a very powerful feature that allows variable inside the Tuple on the left to be assigned values inside the Tuple on the right simultaneously.

For example:

```
(a,b,c,d) = (23,12,73,45)
print(a)
print(b)
print(c)
print(d)
```

Output:

```
23
12
73
45
```

It can be seen that with only the first line of the code, all of 4 variables were assigned values.

How about if we try to assign just 3 values to 4 variables?

```
(a,b,c,d) = (23,12,73)
print(a)
print(b)
print(c)
print(d)
```

Output:

4 variables on the left side can never match with 3 values on the right side. Therefore, the number of variables on the left and the number of values on the right have to be equal.

• What is Dictionary?

String, Lists, and Tuples are data types we have studied so far, which are ordered collections. In other words, we can access items inside collections by locating index positions.

Dictionaries are different. They are unordered and associative collections containing keys and values. In Python, Dictionary maps an immutable key to a value that can be any data type.

This is how a dictionary looks like:

{"totti":10, "carlos":6, "maldini":3, "ramos":4}

In this Dictionary, keys are players' names which are mapped to their associative numbers on jerseys.

Another example of Dictionary:

{"France" : "Paris", "Italy" : "Rome", "Germany" : "Berlin", "Spain" : "Madrid", "Japan" : "Tokyo"}

In this Dictionary, keys are names of countries which are mapped to their associative capitals.

Additionally, another way to create a dictionary is to start with the empty dictionary and then add key-value pairs.

For example:

```
numbers = {}
numbers["one"] = 1
numbers["two"] = 2
numbers["three"] = 3
numbers["four"] = 4
print(numbers)
```

Output:

```
{'one': 1, 'two': 2, 'three': 3, 'four': 4}
```

This is how a dictionary looks. Strings such as "one", "two", "three", and "four" are its keys and Integers 1, 2, 3, and 4 are associative values respectively.

Every key has its associative value. For example:

```
capDict = {"France" : "Paris", "Italy" : "Rome", "Germany" : "Berlin", "Spain" :
"Madrid", "Japan" : "Tokyo"}
print(capDict["Germany"])
```

Output:

```
Berlin
```

In this example, a dictionary named capDict was declared on the first line with nations mapped to their associative capitals. "France", "Italy", "Germany", "Spain" and "Japan" are keys, and "Paris", "Rome", "Berlin", "Madrid" and "Tokyo" are their values respectively. The value of "Germany" is "Berlin", so capDict["Germany"] returns "Berlin" as an output.

1) What is printed by the following statements?

```
numbers = {"one" : 1, "two" : 2, "three" : 3, "four" : 4}

print(numbers["two"])
```

A) two
B) 2
C) three
D) 3

2) What is printed by the following statements?

```
numbers = {"one" : 1, "two" : 2, "three" : 3, "four" : 4}

numbers["two"] = 5

print(numbers["two"] + numbers["three"])
```

A) twothree
B) 5
C) 7
D) 8

✓ Answer:

1) B

The key "two" has its value which is 2, so the output is 2.

2) D

In the original dictionary, the values of "two" and "three" are 2 and 3 respectively. After that, the value of "two" was changed to 5 in the second line. Therefore, numbers["two"] + numbers["three"] = 5 + 3 = 8.

• Dictionary Operation:

First of all, the **in** and **not in** operators can test if a key is in the dictionary.

```
capDict = {"France" : "Paris", "Italy" : "Rome", "Germany" : "Berlin", "Spain" :
"Madrid", "Japan" : "Tokyo"}

print("Italy" in capDict)

print("Rome" in capDict)
```

Ouput:

```
True
False
```

It is noted that "Italy" is a key inside capDict, so the statement "Italy" in capDict is True. However, "Rome" is not a key in capDict although it is a value in this Dictionary, so it still returns False because the **in** operator just cares about the keys, not the values.

In addition, to add values to a Dictionary, we just simply add key-value pairs to the Dictionary declared before.

On the other hand, to delete a key-value pair, we use the **del** statement.

For example:

```
capDict = {"France" : "Paris", "Italy" : "Rome", "Germany" : "Berlin", "Spain" :
"Madrid", "Japan" : "Tokyo"}

capDict["Korea"] = "Seoul"

capDict["Vietnam"] = "Hanoi"

print(capDict)
```

Output:

```
{'France': 'Paris', 'Italy': 'Rome', 'Germany': 'Berlin', 'Spain': 'Madrid', 'Japan':
'Tokyo', 'Korea': 'Seoul', 'Vietnam': 'Hanoi'}
```

It can be seen that 2 key-value pairs "Korea" : "Seoul" and "Vietnam" : "Hanoi" were added to the end of the Dictionary capDict.

Now, let's start deleting some key-value pairs:

```
capDict = {"France" : "Paris", "Italy" : "Rome", "Germany" : "Berlin", "Spain" :
"Madrid", "Japan" : "Tokyo"}

capDict["Korea"] = "Seoul"

capDict["Vietnam"] = "Hanoi"

del capDict["Germany"]

del capDict["France"]

del capDict["Spain"]

print(capDict)
```

Output:

```
{'Italy': 'Rome', 'Japan': 'Tokyo', 'Korea': 'Seoul', 'Vietnam': 'Hanoi'}
```

Now, three keys "Germany", "France" and "Spain" were removed from the Dictionary with their values.

✎ Check Your Understanding:

What is printed by the following statements?

```
dicty = {"a":4, "b":16, "c":93}

dicty["d"] = dicty["a"] + dicty["b"]

print(dicty)
```

A) {'a': 4, 'b': 16, 'c': 93}
B) {'a': 4, 'b': 16, 'c': 93, 'd': 'ab'}
C) {'a': 4, 'b': 16, 'c': 93, 'd': 20}
D) Error

✓ C is the correct answer. The key "d" was added to the dicty at the second line. Its value equals the sum of the value of key "a" and the value of key "b", so the value of the key "d" is 4 + 16 = 20. Therefore, they key-value pair "d": 20 was added to the Dictionary dicty in this code.

• Dictionary Methods:

There are a lot of Dictionary methods built in Python. However, in this book, we just mention some of them, which are useful and suitable for those who start learning to code.

To discover and learn more about Dictionary methods, you can visit the website docs.python.org

Supposed we have a Dictionary called d. Here are some methods of Dictionary:

- **d.keys()** – Returns all the keys in that Dictionary.
- **d.values()** – Returns all the values in that Dictionary.
- **d.items()** – Returns all the key-value pairs in that Dictionary.
- **d.get(key)** – Returns the value associated with that key in the Dictionary or returns None otherwise.
- **s.get(key,other)** – Returns the value associated with that key in the Dictionary or returns other if that key is not in the Dictionary.

For example:

```
capDict = {"France" : "Paris", "Italy" : "Rome", "Germany" : "Berlin", "Spain" :
"Madrid", "Japan" : "Tokyo"}

print(capDict.keys())

print(capDict.values())
```

Output:

```
['France', 'Italy', 'Germany', 'Spain', 'Japan']

['Paris', 'Rome', 'Berlin', 'Madrid', 'Tokyo']
```

It can be seen that capDict.keys() returned a List containing all the keys in capDict
which are 'France', 'Italy', 'Germany', 'Spain', and 'Japan'. On the other hand,
capDict.values() returned all the associated values which are 'Paris', 'Rome',
'Berlin', 'Madrid', and 'Tokyo'.

We learned that d.items() will return all key-value pairs in the Dictionary. Because
printing the Dictionary also shows all key-value pairs, what is difference between
printing out d.items() and printing out the Dictionary d itself?

```
capDict = {"France" : "Paris", "Italy" : "Rome", "Germany" : "Berlin", "Spain" :
"Madrid", "Japan" : "Tokyo"}

print(capDict)

print(capDict.items())
```

Output:

```
{'France': 'Paris', 'Italy': 'Rome', 'Germany': 'Berlin', 'Spain': 'Madrid', 'Japan':
'Tokyo'}

[('France', 'Paris'), ('Italy', 'Rome'), ('Germany', 'Berlin'), ('Spain', 'Madrid'),
('Japan', 'Tokyo')]
```

Although both ways can print out all the key-value pairs in the Dictionary, the ways they print out are different. Printing capDict itself just returns a Dictionary, while capDict.items() returns a List of elements, and each elements are a pair of key-value.

Now, let's take a look at an example about get() methods:

```
capDict = {"France" : "Paris", "Italy" : "Rome", "Germany" : "Berlin", "Spain" :
"Madrid", "Japan" : "Tokyo"}

print(capDict.get("Italy"))

print(capDict.get("Finland"))

print(capDict.get("Finland", "Helsinki"))

print(capDict)
```

Output:

```
Rome
None
Helsinki
{'France': 'Paris', 'Italy': 'Rome', 'Germany': 'Berlin', 'Spain': 'Madrid', 'Japan':
'Tokyo'}
```

Using get() method to find the values of "Italy", we get "Rome". However, when we try to get the value of "Finland", it returns None as "Finland" is not a key in our Dictionary. At the next line, we put "Helsinki" as an alternative result in the case that "Finland" is not a key so that the result we will get is not None anymore. Finally, the last line in the code is just for checking if the key-value pair "Finland"-"Helsinki" was added to the Dictionary capDict or not. The answer is No.

✎ Check Your Understanding:

1) What is printed by the following statements?

```
dicty = {"a":16, "b":4, "c":9, "d":3}
e = dicty.get("c") / dicty.get("b")
print(e)
```

A) cb
B) 2.25
C) 2
D) Error

2) What is printed by the following code?

```
dicty = {"a":16, "b":4, "c":9, "d":3}
e = dicty.values()
f = e[2]
print(f)
```

A) [16, 4, 9, 3]
B) [9, 3]
C) f
D) 9

✓ Answer:

1) B

Because the values of "c" and "b" are 9 and 4 respectively, dicty.get("c") / dicty.get("b") means 9 / 4. Therefore, the output is 2.25.

2) D

From the code above, e is a list of values collected from dicty, so e is [16, 4, 9, 3]. The next line shows that f is the item at the index position 2 of the list e. Therefore, f equals 9, which is also the result expected.

• Dictionary & Alias:

Both Lists and Dictionaries are mutable, so we also need to learn about alias, the topic we mentioned before in the Chapter 4.

Remember in Lists, if two variables refer to the same List, changes to one List can affect the other. Same with Dictionary:

```
cities = {"Richmond": "Virginia", "Austin" : "Texas", "Rochester" : "New York"}

alias = cities

print(alias is cities)

alias["Rochester"] = "Minnesota"

print(cities["Rochester"])
```

Output:

```
True

Minnesota
```

It can be seen that when we try to modify the Dictionary alias in the code above, the Dictionary cities is also affected. This is because they are refer to the same object.

We can understand alias as a deep copy of cities. However, we can also make a shallow copy for cities.

```
cities = {"Richmond": "Virginia", "Austin" : "Texas", "Rochester" : "New York"}

aCopy = cities.copy()

print(aCopy is cities)

aCopy["Rochester"] = "Minnesota"

print(cities["Rochester"])
```

Output:

False
New York

Now, the variable aCopy is just a shallow copy from the Dictionary cities, so any change in aCopy does not affect the original Dictionary. That's why the statement aCopy is cities is False as they do not refer to the same object. Furthermore, the value of "Rochester" in aCopy becomes "Minnesota", but the value of "Rochester" in the original Dictionary is still unchanged.

🐇 Check Your Understanding:

What is printed by the following statements?

```
dictA = {"a" : 1, "b" : 2, "c" : 3, "d" : 4}
dictB = dictA
dictC = dictA.copy()
dictB["b"] = "two"
print(dictA["b"])
```

A) 2
B) two
C) 3
D) three

✓ B is the correct answer because dictB is a deep copy of dictA. It means any change in dictB also affects dictA. That's why dictB["b"] = "two" also changes the value of "b" in dictA to "two". Therefore, "two" is our expected output.

🖐 Chapter Review Questions:

1) Tuples are immutable. True or False?

2) What is printed by the code below?

```
numbers = {"a" : 12, "b" : 7, "c" : 23, "d" : 15}

numbers["b"] = 21

print(numbers["b"] + numbers["c"])
```

A) bc
B) 30
C) 44
D) 28

3) What is printed by the code below?

```
dicty = {"a":2, "b":5, "c":6, "d":9}

e = dicty.keys()

f = e[1]

print(f)
```

A) 2
B) 5
C) b
D) a

4) What is printed by the code below?

```
dictA = {"a" : 6, "b" : 2, "c" : 5, "d" : 9}

dictB = dictA

dictC = dictA.copy()

dictB["b"] = "7"

print(dictA["b"])
```

A) b
B) 2
C) 5
D) 7

5) What is printed by the code below?

```
dicty = {"a":2, "b":5, "c":6, "d":9}
e = dicty.values()
f = e[1] + e[2]
print(f)
```

A) 3
B) 7
C) 11
D) bc

✓ **Solutions:**

1) True

2) C

3) C

4) D

5) C

CHAPTER 6: FLOW CONTROL

This chapter is designed to help you understand and control well the flow of code, which includes a lot of different parts. Controlling well the coding flow enable us to solve complicated problems more efficiently.

First of all, if we are going to make a decision in a program, we are going to need conditional statements.

• Conditional Statements:

Conditional statements enable us to check the conditions and choose the way we want to go. In other words, this can be understood as a binary selection since there are two possible paths of execution.

    o **if** statement:

Structure:

```
if <condition> :
    <then do something>
```

The word **if** is followed by some conditions, and we put a colon : after it. The statement below is indented inside of this if statement. It means the part <then do something> is still a part of the if statement because it is indented inside of them.

For example:

```
if 2 < 3:
    print("Yes")
```

Output:

```
Yes
```

Because 2 < 3 is True, the third line of code is executed. Therefore, the output is printed out Yes. (If the second line is not indented inside, you will see Error.)

- o **if – else** statement:

Structure:

```
if <condition>:

    <then do something if condition is met>

else:

    <do something else if condition is not met>
```

Be careful with indentation. The **else** needs to line up with the **if** to let Python know where the **else** belongs.

For example:

```
a = 5

if a > 7 :

    print("a is greater than 7")

else:

    print("NOT greater than 7")
```

Output:

```
NOT greater than 7
```

It can be seen that a is equal 5, so a > 7 is False. That's why the third line is not executed and "a is greater than 7" is not printed out. Because the condition is not met, the flow jumped into **else**, and the fifth statement is executed.

○ **elif** statement:

```
if <condition 1 is met> :
   <do A>
elif <condition 2 is met> :
   <do B>
elif <condition 3 is met> :
   <do C>
else:
   <do D>
```

The **elif** stands for "else if" and you can have as many elif statements as you like. All the **if, elif,** and **else** must be line up with each other. Indentation is extremely important in Python because anything intended works as a block of coded that gets executed if the condition is met.

For example:

```
a = -2
if a > 0:
   print("a is positive")
elif a < 0:
   print("a is negative")
else:
   print("neither positive nor negative")
```

Output:

a is negative

The output is printed out as "a is negative" because -2 < 0 and the condition in the **elif** statement is met. It is noted that if you put a = 5, "a is positive" will be the output. If you put a = 0, "neither positive or negative" will be printed out. That's how it works.

    ✎ Check Your Understanding:

What is printed by the following statements?

```
a = 23
b = 4
if a % b == 0:
    print(0)
elif a % b == 1:
    print(1)
elif a % b == 2:
    print(2)
else:
    print(3)
```

    A) 0
    B) 1
    C) 2
    D) 3

    ✓ D is the correct answer. 23 % 4 = 3 because 3 is the remainder when 23 is divided by 4. Because the result is not 0, 1 or 2, the statement inside the **else** get executed and 3 is printed out as an expected output.

It is noted that one conditional statement can be nested within another. You can realize that it is completely possible that after making a decision, we can face another decision to make. That's why many if statements can be nested inside other if statements.

Let's take this situation for example: we want to check if -4 is an even negative number. First, we have to check if it's a positive number, a negative number or none of them. After that, if the number is negative, the second decision to make is that number is an odd or even number. Therefore, it can be seen that there are two decisions to make, so nested if statements are needed to solve this problem. This is how we demonstrate this situation in Python code:

```python
a = -4
if a > 0:
    if a % 2 == 0:
        print("a is an even positive number")
    else:
        print("a is an odd positive number")
elif a < 0:
    if a % 2 == 0:
        print("a is an even negative number")
    else:
        print("a is an odd negative number")
else:
    print("a is neither positive nor negative")
```

Output:

a is an even negative number

In the code, a is -4. -4 is less than 0, so at the first decision, it decides to go inside the elif a < 0 condition. Next, we have to decide -4 is an odd or even number inside this conditional statement. Because -4 is an even number, the flow goes into if a % 2 == 0, and then print("a is an even negative number") get executed.

✎ Check Your Understanding:

What is printed when the following statements execute?

```
if 5 > 3:
    if 9 < 7:
        print("Yes! That's right!")
    else:
        print("Something wrong...")
else:
    print("Wrong at the first step!")
```

A) Yes! That's right!
B) Something wrong...
C) Wrong at the first step!
D) Error

✓ B is the correct answer because first 5 > 3 is True, so the output must be "Yes! That's right!" or "Something wrong...". At the second decision making, 9 < 7 is False, so the statement "Something wrong..." gets executed.

❖ Coding Challenge:

To solve this question, you must be very good at controlling conditional statements which can be nested inside other ones. Alright, now this is the problem to solve:

Supposed a student takes SAT examination, which includes 3 sections: Math, Critical Reading, and Writing. If the student gets over 600 points for every section, print out "High score in every section!" If the student just get one of them over 600, the output should print out to tell him that section is high such as "High score in Math section!", "High score in Critical Reading section!", or "High score in Writing section!" Additionally, if the student only get one section below 600, tell him he did well in other two sections (ex: "High score in Math and Writing!") Finally, if there is no section above 600, print out "Good luck next time!"

Write your code to ask the users type in their scores and print out the comments like the description above. For example, if the user types 700 for Math and Critical Reading scores and 500 for Writing score, this user will see the message "High score in Math and Critical Reading!"). Use input() we learned in the chapter 2 to help your code.

Some more examples of expected outputs:

Scores	Output
Math: 780, Critical Reading: 680, Writing: 720	High score in every section!
Math: 800, Critical Reading: 520, Writing: 690	High score in Math and Writing!
Math: 500, Critical Reading: 580, Writing: 700	High score in Writing section!
Math: 500, Critical Reading: 480, Writing: 490	Good luck next time!

The answer will be shown on the next page.

```python
math = int(input("Please enter your Math score"))
criticalReading = int(input("Please enter your Critical Reading score"))
writing = int(input("Please enter your Writing score"))
if math > 600:
  if criticalReading > 600:
    if writing > 600:
      print("High score in every section!")
    else:
      print("High score in Math and Critical Reading!")
  else:
    if writing > 600:
      print("High score in Math and Writing!")
    else:
      print("High score in Math section!")
else:
  if criticalReading > 600:
    if writing > 600:
      print("High score in Critical Reading and Writing!")
    else:
      print("High score in Critical Reading section!")
  else:
    if writing > 600:
      print("High score in Writing section!")
    else:
      print("Good luck next time!")
```

• The FOR loops:

The loops in general are designed to support iteration, which is repeated execution of a sequence of statements. In this book, we introduce you two loops: the **for** loop and the **while** loop.

In Python, the **for** loop statement allows us to implement iteration. We will show you how to use for loop in range, in a String and in a List.

o The **for** loop in range:

First of all, let's take a look at the for loop in range. This is the structure:

> **for** something **in range**(numerical range):

The words **for** and **in range** are required and you cannot change it, but the word "something" is just a variable name, so it doesn't matter if you change that name. Noticeably, you should put a valid range which contains numbers inside the parentheses. If you but a String or List in this case, it won't work.

For example:

```
for anum in range(5):
    print(anum)
```

Output:

```
0
1
2
3
4
```

The first line of code hints that anum is in the range(5), which includes integers from 0 to 4 (again, Computer Scientists love to count from 0, and 5 is not included). That's why all numbers from 0 to 4 are printed out in every line.

How about if we don't want to start at 0? That's alright because you can put the starting point like this:

```
for anum in range(1,5):
   print(anum)
```

Output:

```
1
2
3
4
```

It can be seen clearly now that there are two numbers in parentheses instead of just one number like the previous example. The first number is the starting point and the second number is the limit, which is not included.

Can we put 3 numbers inside the parentheses? Yes, we can put up to 3 things inside the range. For example:

```
for anum in range(1,10,2):
   print(anum)
```

Output:

```
1
3
5
7
9
```

The output says it all. The range starts at 1 and goes up to 9 (10 is not included), and anum increases by 2 every time it goes to the next value. In other words, 2 is the increment in the range.

All of the three examples above printed out a sequence of numbers from smallest to largest numbers. The question is "Can we count a sequence number backward?" For example, can we count down a sequence from 5 to 1 (5, 4, 3, 2, 1) instead of counting up from 1 to 5 (1, 2, 3, 4, 5)? Let's try it with setting up the starting point and the end point equal 5 and 0 respectively (0 is not included as usual so 1 will be reached), so the range we will use is range(5,0). It makes some sense, right? Now, look at an example below:

```
for anum in range(5,0):
    print(anum)
```

Output:

The output is not what we expected. Nothing is printed out because what Python understand in this case is there is no number that less than 0 but greater than 5.

By default, Python considers a range numbers counted up by 1 if you don't put a specific increment into the parentheses. This is how we solve this problem:

```
for anum in range(5,0,-1):
    print(anum)
```

Output:

```
5
4
3
2
1
```

Now everything makes more sense, right? Because the increment is -1, anum decreases by 1 every time it goes to the next value in the loop. Therefore, starting from 5, anum decreases steadily to 4, 3, 2, and 1 at the end of the loop as 0 is set as the boundary of the loop.

🖐 Check Your Understanding:

To have the desired output below, what is the right code to run?

```
10
8
6
4
2
```

A) for anum in range(10,1,-2):
        print(anum)

B) for anum in range(10,0,2):
        print(anum)

C) for anum in range(1,10,-2):
        print(anum)

D) for anum in range(10,2,-2):
        print(anum)

✓ A is the correct answer. The sequence starts from 10 then it goes down to 2 (1 is not included). Every time anum gets to the next value, it decreases by 2 as the increment we put in is -2.

○ The **for** loop in String:

The way the **for** loop works in String is simpler than it does in range. This is the structure:

```
for something in theString:
```

The words **for** and **in** are required in the statement, but the word "something" and "theString" you see in the Structure are just variable names. Now a String or a variable which has type String should be placed inside the parentheses. If you put a number is this case, it won't work.

For example:

```
for achar in "hello":
    print(achar)
```

Output:

```
h
e
l
l
o
```

In this loop, achar is values which are characters taken from the String "hello".

The for loop in a String simply takes all the characters of that String.

We also can use a variable to place after **in** as long as its type is String.

```
say = "hello"
for achar in say:
    print(achar)
```

Output:

```
h
e
l
l
o
```

In this code, the variable say is declared as a String, so we still can put it after the word **in** at the for statement and it works the same way as the previous example.

✎ Check Your Understanding:

What is printed by the following statements?

```
for i in "oh yes" :
  print(i)
```

A) oh yes

B) ohyes

C) o
   h
   y
   e
   s

D) o
   h

   y
   e
   s

✓ D is the correct answer. First, every character taken from the String is printed in every line, not in one line. Second, the blank space is also a character in the String, so it is supposed to be printed out. That's why D is the expected output from the code above.

o The **for** loop in List:

The way **for** loop works in List is very similar to it does in String. This is the structure:

```
for something in theList:
```

Similarly, the words **for** and **in** are required in the statement, but the word "something" and "theList" you see are just variable names. Also, a List or a variable which has type List can be placed inside the parentheses. If you put a number is this case, it won't work. The colon : is also required for syntax.

For example:

```
for item in [1,2,3,4]:
    print(item)
```

Output:

```
1
2
3
4
```

In this loop, item is elements from the List [1,2,3,4]. The for loop in List helps to access to every single element in a List. That's why 1, 2, 3, and 4 are accessed and printed out as output in every line.

A variable is also can be placed after the word **in** as long as it's a List.

For example:

```
myList = [1,2,3,4]
for item in myList:
   print(item)
```

Output:

```
1
2
3
4
```

Similar to the previous example, this code also prints out all elements in myList, which refers to the List [1, 2, 3, 4]. This is a more recommended way to do with the for loop.

✎ Check Your Understanding:

Which following code has no error?

A) for i in range["a","b","c",1,2]:
      print(i)

B) for i in ["a","b","c",1,2]
      print(i)

C) for i in ["a","b","c",1,2]:
      print(i)

D) for item in ["a","b","c",1,2]:
      print(i)

✓ C is the correct answer. Choice A should not have the word "range" there; choice B lacks of the colon : at the end of line 1; choice D has problem with variable names (i and item). Finally, choice C fulfills all syntax requirements.

❖ Coding Challenge:

Use for loop to write a program that outputs numbers from 1 to 10. However, for even numbers, it should output "ye" instead of the number and for the multiples of three output "yay". The output should look like this:

```
1
ye
yay
ye
5
ye
7
ye
yay
ye
```

✓ Answer:

```
for i in range(1,11):
    if i % 2 == 0:
        print("ye")
    elif i % 3 == 0:
        print("yay")
    else:
        print(i)
```

• The WHILE loops:

Besides the **for** loop, the **while** loop also helps us build iteration in Python. The ways **for** loop and **while** loop work are slightly different, but they both use limit condition to control the flow of execution. It is noted that the body of while loop will be repeated until the condition is no longer True. Thanks to this, the **while** loop is sometimes even more flexible than the for loop in some cases.

We already know how to use the **for** loop to access and print out numbers from 1 to 5. Now, let's do the same job with **while** loop:

```
anum = 1
while (anum <= 5):
    print(anum)
    anum = anum + 1
```

Output:

```
1
2
3
4
5
```

The output is exactly as expected: we printed out 1, 2, 3, 4, 5 by using the while loop. First, let's declare a variable named anum equals 1 to start. Next, the second line in the code means the condition is anum is less than or equal 5. In other words, as long as anum does not exceed 5, stuffs inside the while loop keeps flowing. Therefore, 1 is printed out first because the condition is True at the moment. After that, the last line updates anum by adding 1, so anum becomes 2. 2 is still less than 5, so 2 is printed out and updated to 3 after that. The process keeps moving forward until anum becomes 6 because 6 is no longer less than or equal 5. Thus, 1, 2, 3, 4, 5 is printed out before the while loop ends.

The **while** loop is flexible, but trade-off happens sometimes. It is when the while loop is not well designed and everything gets stuck in an indefinite loop. It means the loop will repeat forever because it never knows where and when to stop running.

What happens if we take out the last line of the code above?

```
anum = 1
while (anum <= 5):
    print(anum)
```

Output:

```
1
1
1
1
1
1
.
.
.
(frozen)
```

This code is very bad because the loop keeps running forever, making your computer frozen for a while. It is because the last line was removed, so anum is not updated to the next value anymore. In other words, anum in this code is always 1. 1 is never greater than 5, so the loop never ends. The while loop just stops until the condition is no longer True. So be careful!

The **while** loop still gets stuck sometimes even though we update the value. This is an example:

```
anum = 1
while (anum % 2 == 1):
    print(anum)
    anum = anum + 2
```

Output:

```
1
3
5
7
9
11
13
.

.

.
(frozen)
```

The loop in this code also keeps running forever even though anum is updated to the next values at the last line. This is because the condition is always True even though anum keeps changing. In this case, the loop just stops if anum is an even number because the while loop keeps running as long as anum is an odd number (an odd number divided by 2 always produces the remainder 1). Unfortunately, anum can never be even because it increases by 2 all the time, making a sequence of odd numbers 1, 3, 5, 7, 9, 11, 13, 15, 17,... That's why this is another infinite loop.

The body of the loop should change the value of one or more variables so that eventually the condition becomes False and the loop terminates. Otherwise the loop will repeat forever. This is called an infinite loop. An endless source of amusement for computer scientists is the observation that the directions written on the back of the shampoo bottle (lather, rinse, repeat) create an infinite loop.

✍ Check Your Understanding:

Which code below will print out even numbers from 0 to 10 (0 and 10 are included)?

```
A) anum = 0
   while (anum < 10):
       print(anum)
       anum = anum + 2
```

```
B) anum = 0
   while (anum < 11):
       print(anum)
       anum = anum + 2
```

```
C) anum = 0
   while (anum < 11):
       anum = anum + 2
       print(anum)
```

```
D) anum = 0
   while (anum < 11):
       print(anum)
```

✓ B is the correct answer. It can be clearly seen that the choice A does not include number 10, while the choice C does not include 0. The choice D is an infinite loop.

• Branching Statements:

We've now covered most of the flow controlling in Python. Next, let's move to branching statements topic, which is very useful to know to control your coding flow efficiently. In this topic, we will talk about 2 important key words of branching statement: **break** and **continue.**

  o **break**:

The **break** statement causes the program to exit a loop when a certain condition is met without waiting for the loop to finish.

Let's see how the **break** statement works to print out 1, 2, 3, 4, 5 like previous examples did:

```
anum = 1
while True:
   print(anum)
   if anum == 5:
     break
   anum = anum + 1
```

Output:

```
1
2
3
4
5
```

It looks very similar to what we did with the **while** loop before. We set up anum equals 1 at the beginning and keep updating by adding 1 to anum. However, instead of putting the condition at the beginning of the while loop, we choose to put it inside the while loop. Thanks to a conditional statement applied, the **break** statement is used to exit the loop when anum becomes 5. That's why the code prints numbers from 1 to 5 because when anum equals 5, the loop stops and there is no more update.

Some of students question why we need to use **break** statement when we can solve the problem without it like examples we learned before. This is actually a good question. To answer this, try to solve this problem.

❖ Coding Challenge:

Question: Find the 30th prime number.

Explanation: As we know, a prime number is divisible just by 1 and itself. Supposed the first prime number is 2, the second prime number is 3, and the third prime number is 5, then we have a sequence of prime numbers like this 2, 3, 5, 7, 11, 13... What is the 30th prime number?

We cannot calculate the 30th prime number just as easily as calculate the 30th even number. It is because the difference between every consecutive even numbers is always 2, but the difference between every prime number is not stable. This leads to a trouble: we cannot determine the destination if using the for loop.

Do you think we need the **break** statement to solve this?

The answer is on the next page. But first, try your best to solve this problem.

Good luck!

✓ Answer:

```
num = 2
count = 0
while True:
    prime = True
    for i in range(2,num):
        if num % i == 0:
            prime = False
    if prime:
        count = count + 1
    if count == 30:
        print(num)
        break
    num = num + 1
```

This coding challenge now is more complicated than problems we have done so far. The first line lets us know that num starts at 1, and the last line makes sure num is updated every turn in the loop. The variable count is declared to keep track the order number of prime number, so it was 0 at the beginning because there is no prime number found before the while loop. The line 3 of the code while True: means the loop will keep running until we want to exit at some special point. In other words, it just stops when we **break** it, so we will break it at the 30th prime number.

Noticeably, the for loop used inside is for checking if num is a prime number or not. The rule is simple, first we assume the number is a prime number by declaring prime = True at line 4. However, if that number can be divisible by any other number besides 1 and itself, that number is no longer a prime number and prime = False.

Do not forget to keep track on the order number of prime number whenever we found a prime number. That's why we keep adding 1 to count whenever prime is True, and if prime is False, then we don't need to. Finally, when we reach the 30th prime number, it means count now equals 30, and we print it out. After getting the result we want, we exit the loop by **break** statement.

That's how the **break** work in the flow of program.

o **continue:**

The **continue** keyword makes the flow of code skip at one specific step and jump into other steps after that. While the **break** statement makes the loop completely stop, the **continue** statement just skip at one condition and then continue the flow.

Compare these two codes to see the difference between **break** and **continue**:

Code 1:

```
num = 0
while num < 8:
    num = num + 1
    if num == 5:
        break
    print(num)
```

Output:

```
1
2
3
4
```

Code 2:

```
num = 0
while num < 8:
   num = num + 1
   if num == 5:
      continue
   print(num)
```

Output:

```
1
2
3
4
6
7
8
```

The Code 1 and Code 2 above are 99% similar. The only difference between them is in line 5: The Code 1 uses **break**, while the Code 2 uses **continue.** As a result, the outputs now are interestingly different. In the Code 1, when num equals 5, the **break** statement is executed and the program exit the loop immediately before printing 5. That's why the Code 1 just only print 1,2,3 and 4. On the other hand, the **continue** in the Code 2 allows the flow to skip the rest of that case and continue on the next iteration of the loop when num equals 6. After skipping num equals 5, the loop still runs with num equals 6 until num < 8 is no longer True. That's why all numbers from 1 to 8 are printed except 5.

Note: It is noticeable that in this while loop, we write the updating line before printing to avoid being stuck in the loop.

This is the bad code:

```
num = 1
while num < 8:
    print(num)
    if num == 5:
        continue
    num = num + 1
```

Output:

```
1
2
3
4
5
5
5
5
5
.
.
.
(frozen)
```

This code is stuck in an infinite loop, which keeps printing the number 5 forever. The reason is that the updating line num = num + 1 is put after the **continue** statement. The **continue** skips the rest, so num is never updated by adding 1. In other words, num is 5 forever and cannot become 6 to get out of the infinite loop. Therefore, be careful when you work with while loop.

✍ Check Your Understanding:

What is printed by the following statements?

```
for achar in "hello":
  if achar == "l":
    continue
  print(achar)
```

A) h
   e

B) h
   e
   o

C) h
   e
   l
   l
   o

D) (Frozen in an infinite loop)

✓ B is the correct answer because the **continue** skipped all letter "l", so just letters "h", "e", and "o" can be printed out in this case.

• Exception Handlings:

Exceptions appear when errors are detected during execution, disrupting the flow of the program. An exception can be seen as a Python object that represents an error. However, it is noted that although all errors in Python are caught by exceptions, not all exceptions are errors.

When an error happens:

```
print(5 / 0)
```

Output:

```
builtins.ZeroDivisionError: division by zero
```

It can be seen that when an error is detected, an exception appears and a message is printed out to hint us what happened. In this case, Python understands that a number cannot be divided by 0, so it prints out a message to let us know our mistake.

How about if we want to print out messages for some specific errors or conditions we want to set up? To deal with this, we can use **try – except** statements. Here is the structure:

```
try:
    do something
except:
    do something else if errors happen
```

For example:

```
try:
    print(5 / 0)
except:
    print("A number cannot be divided by 0")
```

Output:

```
A number cannot be divided by 0
```

It can be seen from the code above that the print(5 / 0) statement cannot be executed as the error happens. Therefore, the flow jumps into the **except** statement and the last line gets executed.

If we want to demonstrate specific error messages, we can specify the error type after the **except** keyword. For example:

```
try:

    b = int(input("Please enter a number: "))

    print(5 / b)

except ZeroDivisionError:

    print("A number cannot be divided by zero!")

except ValueError:

    print("Please enter a number!")

except Exception as e:

    print("Unknown error", e)
```

If you put 5, the ouput will be:

```
1.0
```

If you put 0, the output will be:

```
A number cannot be divided by zero!
```

If you put "abc", the output will be:

```
Please enter a number!
```

It can be seen that when b equals 5, no error happens so the output is 1.0. However, when we try to divide 5 by 0, the flow will go into the except ZeroDivisionError and execute the fifth line of code, so the statement "A number cannot be divided by zero!" is printed out. On the other hand, if we try to put characters that are not a number, Python will understand this is ValueError and the flow will go into the except ValueError statement. As a result, it says "Please enter a number!" Finally, if there is any other error, the last line will get executed.

The question here is that how can we know key terms such as ZeroDivisionError or ValueError to deal with these kind of codes? Here is the answer. They are called standard exceptions in Python, which can be found in this table:

Exceptions	Description
StopIteration	Raised when the next() method of an iterator fails to point to any object.
SystemExit	Raised by the sys.exit() function.
StandardError	Base class for all built-in exceptions except StopIteration and SystemExit.
ImportError	Raised when some errors happen in an import statement.
SyntaxError	Raised if there is a Python syntax error.
TypeError	Raised when an operation or function is applied to an object of inappropriate type.
IndentationError	Raised when indentation is not performed properly.
NameError	Raised when an identifier is not found.
IndexError	Raised when it fails to find an index in a sequence.
LookupError	Base class for all lookup errors.
UnboundLocalError	Raised when a reference is made to a local variable in a function or method, but no value has been bound to it.
KeyError	Raised when the specified key cannot be found in the dictionary
ValueError	Raised when the built-in function for a data type has the valid type of arguments, but the arguments have invalid values specified.
MemoryError	Raised when a operation runs out of memory.
RuntimeError	Raised when a generated error does not fall into any category.
RecursionError	Raised when it has exceeded the maximum recursion depth.
SystemError	Raised when an internal problem is found, but when this error is encountered the Python interpreter does not exit.

Exceptions	Description
ArithmeticError	Base class for all errors that occur for numeric calculation in case you do not know a Math specific error.
ZeroDivisonError	Raised when trying to divide numbers by zero.
OverflowError	Raised when a calculation exceeds limit for a numeric type.
FloatingPointError	Raised when a floating point calculation fails.
IOError	Raised when an input/ output operation fails.
EOFError	Raised when one of the built-in functions hits an EOF, end-of-life, without reading any data.
FileNotFoundError	Raised when a requested file or directory doesn't exist.
PermissionError	Raised when trying to run an operation without the adequate access rights.
KeyboardInterrupt	Raised when the user interrupts program execution.
AssertionError	Raised in case of failure of the Assert statement.
OSError	Raises for operating system related errors.
EnvironmentError	Base class for all exceptions that occur outside the Python environment.
AttributeError	Raised in case of failure of an attribute reference or assignment.
NonimplementedError	Raised when an abstract method that needs to be implemented in an inherited class is not actually implemented.
Exception	Base class for all exceptions. This catches most exception messages.

You can check more types of Exceptions and their hierarchy at
https://docs.python.org/2/library/exceptions.html

In Python, besides using try-except block, you can create an exception message by using the **raise** keyword.

The simplest way to use the raise statement is putting the keyword **raise** followed by the name of an exception.

Structure:

raise ExceptionName(Message)

For example:

```
a = int(input("put the day you get pay every month: "))
if a > 31:
    raise ValueError("The number cannot be greater than 31")
else:
    print (a)
```

When you put 5 as an input:

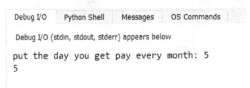

When you put 33 as an input:

The output of this code is very interesting. It shows that we can decide where and when to raise an Exception with our own message. In this case, we require the input is an Integer lower or equal to 31. When the input value received doesn't match with our requirement, a message is printed out to hint the user the error he made. This is very interesting.

✍️ Chapter Review Questions:

1) Write a program to print out numbers from 1 to 100 (including). For the even numbers, the code should print out "even" instead of the number. The output should look like this:

2) Use just two lines of code to print the output like this:

(Hint: The for loop helps!)

3) Use just two lines of code to give the output like below:

4) Use less than 5 lines of code to print the output like this:

Debug I/O   Python Shell   Messages   OS Commands

Debug I/O (stdin, stdout, stderr) appears below

* * * * *   _____
* * * * *   _____
* * * * *   _____
* * * * *   _____

             _____
             _____
             _____
             _____

(You don't need to force yourself print exactly same as this. 80% similar to this is good enough.)

5) Write a program to calculate the sum of natural numbers from 1 to 100 (including). In other words, calculate 1 + 2 + 3 + 4 + ... + 97 + 98 + 99 + 100. (Hint: 5050 is the answer!)

6) Write a program to count how many numbers that divisible by 7 from 1 to 100. (Hint: There are 14 numbers from 1 to 100 divisible by 7.)

7) Write a program that prints the numbers from 1 to 100. But for multiples of 3 print "Fizz" instead of the number and for the multiples of 5 print "Buzz". For numbers which are multiples of both 3 and 5 print "FizzBuzz".

(*) Check solutions on the next page after trying your best!

✓ Solutions:

1)

```
for i in range(1,101):
    if i % 2 == 0:
        print("even")
    else:
        print(i)
```

2)

```
for i in range(5):
    print("*" * 5)
```

3)

```
for i in range(5):
    print(" " * (4-i) + "*" * (i*2+1))
```

4)

```
for i in range(1,5):
    print("* " * 5 + "_" * 15)
for i in range(4):
    print("_" * 25)
```

5)

```
mysum = 0
for i in range(1,101):
    mysum = mysum + i
print(mysum)
```

6)

```
count = 1
for i in range(1,101):
    if i % 7 == 0:
        count = count + 1
print(count)
```

7)

```
for i in range(1,101):
    if i % 3 == 0 and i % 5 == 0:
        print("Fizzbuzz")
    elif i % 3 == 0:
        print("Fizz")
    elif i % 5 == 0:
        print("Buzz")
    else:
        print(i)
```

CHAPTER 7: MODULES

A module is a Python source file, which can expose classes, functions and global variables to help in other Python programs. To use a module, we have to **import** it first. For example:

import math

import turtle

import fibo

import random

Why do we need Modules? It is noted that all definitions we made will be lost when we quit from the Python interpreter. To support this, Python has a way to put definitions in a file and use them in a script. In other words, modules give you tools to support and solve some problems more efficiently.

Python gives to users a lot of different modules which can be found at this link:

https://docs.python.org/3/py-modindex.html

Despite many modules available to use, in this book, we just mention the Math module and the Random module as examples to help you understand more about modules and how they work in Python.

• The Math Module:

The Math module provides mathematical functions and constants that we can use for our code as long as we import math.

There are more information about Math Module available that you can check on this link: https://docs.python.org/3.7/library/math.html#module-math

First, the Math module provides mathematical constants. For example:

```
import math

print(math.pi)

print(math.e)
```

Output:

```
3.14159265359

2.71828182846
```

The output shows that as long as the Math module is imported, Python understand and provides us the pi and e numbers when we need them. The first line of output is the pi number, and the second line shows the e number.

Besides constants, mathematical functions and calculations are also supported by the Math module:

```
import math

print(math.sqrt(4))

print(math.sqrt(3))

print(math.sin(math.radians(90)))

print(math.cos(math.radians(180)))
```

Output:

2.0
1.73205080757
1.0
-1.0

The square root of 4 and 3 are demonstrated by the statement math.sqrt(4) and math.sqrt(3) respectively. As expected, 2.0 is the result of the square root of 4, and the square root of 3 is around 1.732. Furthermore, sin(math.radians(90)) and cos(math.radians(180)) displays the sin of 90 degrees and cos of 180 degree, which equal 1.0 and -1.0 respectively. The Math module in Python understands and provides exactly what we want as long as we import it. All of these values can be checked again with calculator.

✌ Check Your Understanding:

What is printed by the following statements:

```
import math
a = math.sqrt(4)
b = (math.sin(math.radians(90)))
print(int(a-b))
```

A) 1
B) 1.0
C) 2.0
D) -1

A is the correct anwer. Thanks to the Math module, math.sqrt(4) is 2.0 and math.sin(math.radians(90)) is 1.0. Therefore, a – b equals 1.0, but the statement int(a-b) makes it become 1, an interger.

• The Random Module:

The name says it all: The Random Module enables us to pick random numbers from a specific condition. All the random numbers have an equal probability of occurring. This is very useful in some particular problems to solve such as shuffling a deck of cards or a list of songs.

By default, random.random() will choose randomly a number between 0 and 1. It is noted that a number from 0 to 1 represents probability of a chance, so it cannot be greater than 1 or less than 0. For example:

```
import random

x = random.random()

print(x)
```

Output:

```
0.13026455303
```

If you run this code multiple times, you may get different numbers between 0 and 1 as the number is chosen randomly. Your output is not necessarily exactly same as my output.

Can we choose a number that can be greater than 1 or less than 0? Try random.randrange() !

```
import random

a = random.randrange(1, 9)

b = random.randrange(-9, 0)

print(a)

print(b)
```

Output:

6
-2

Now, it is clear that we can pick a number greater than 1 or less than 0. The randrange() function creates an integer in the given range, which includes not the upper bound but the lower bound.

🖎 Check Your Understanding:

Which answer below can be an output if the following statements get executed?

```
import random
numA = random.random()
numB = numA * 5
print(numB)
```

A) 5.34815481325
B) -3.3421414213
C) 1.71378258915
D) -1.2412412421

✓ C is the correct answer. In the code above, numA has to be a number between 0 and 1. Therefore, first, numA cannot be a negative number, so numB cannot be a negative number neither. That's why choice B and D are wrong. Besides, numA cannot exceed 1, so number cannot exceed 5 neither (numb = numA * 5). Thus, C is the correct answer because 1.71378258915 is between 1 and 5, the range that numB is supposed to be.

✍ Chapter Review Questions:

1) Use for loop to print 10 random numbers between 0 and 1.

2) Print 10 random numbers between 25 and 35, inclusive. Remember the output should be not just integers but any number between 25 and 35 like this:

3) Print 5 random results from throwing a dice.

4) Print 5 random percent values with nice format.

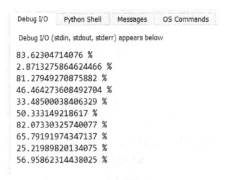

5) Write a program to calculate a perimeter and area of a circle. Ask the user to put the value for radius.

✓ Solutions:

1)

```
import random
for i in range(10):
    ranNum = random.random()
    print(ranNum)
```

2)

```
import random
for i in range(10):
    ranNum = random.random()
    print(25+ ranNum*10)
```

3)

```
import random
for i in range(10):
    ranNum = random.randrange(1,7)
    print(ranNum)
```

4)

```
import random
for i in range(10):
    ranNum = random.random()
    print(ranNum*100, "%")
```

5)

```
import math
radius = int(input("Put the radius value: "))
piNum = math.pi
area = radius ** 2 * piNum
perimeter = radius * 2 * piNum
print("The area: ", area, "\n", "The perimeter: ", perimeter)
```

CHAPTER 8: FUNCTIONS

• What is Function?

A function is a block of organized code used to perform some tasks. Statements like print() or len() that we have learned and used are examples and they all are built-in functions in Python, but you can also create your own functions. It is noted that functions provide better modularity and a high degree of code reusing.

This is the syntax for a function and how it looks like:

```
def functionName(parameters):
    statements
```

The word **def** is required to create a function. On the other hand, functionName can be anything you want to name as long as it makes sense with the task. For instance, the len() function calculates the length of a String or List, and the sum() function sums up all the numbers.

Besides the key word **def**, (parameters) and the colon : are also important and necessary parts of a function. Parameters can be considered as materials needed to make a function perform its task. For example, materials needed to make a kite are wooden dowels, plastic sheeting, strong tape and kite string. Similarly, to make a sum() function to sum up 3 numbers, we need three numbers as materials. If we just put 1 or 2 numbers as parameters in parentheses, then we don't have enough material to make it. Generally, some functions need zero, 1, 2, or even more parameters.

Statements belonged to the function must be indented inside the function. The key word **return** is usually used in this part, but not always. Here is an example of a function that doesn't use the **return** keyword and has no parameter also:

```
def nono():

    print("a")

    print("b")

    print("c")
```

Output:

If you run this code, the output will show nothing as we just wrote the function but did not call it to perform. The nono() function has no parameter and no **return** statement as you can see. All of its job is just printing out "a", "b", and "c" in every line without returning any value.

So how can we call a function to see how it works?

```
def nono():

    print("a")

    print("b")

    print("c")

nono()
```

Output

```
a

b

c
```

When the function is called, it performs its task. In this case, the nono() function is supposed to print out "a", "b", and "c" in every line. Therefore, the output shows exactly what the nono() function performed.

The nono() function does not have parameter, so we do not need to give it the "material" when we call it. To call functions like nono(), we just type its name and parentheses. Remember NOT to include the **def** key word at the beginning and the colon : at the end of statement as we just need them to declare, not to call.

So how to declare and call a function with parameter?

```
def callName(aName):

    print("My name is", aName)


callName("John")

callName("Steve")
```

Output:

```
My name is John

My name is Steve
```

The function callName() is created with one parameter placed inside the parentheses, and this parameter is called aName. This function is made just to print out the name we put in. In this code, we call the function twice: The first time we put a String "John" as a parameter; The second time we put a String "Steve" in a similar way. It means the variable aName inside the function will be assigned to "John" and "Steve", creating the output as expected.

• Function That Return Values:

Most functions are designed to return values. These functions yield return values that we can store and use instead of None. Functions that return values are called fruitful functions, which create actual products to be used. We can see functions are like machines.

For example, if we want to make a machine that add two numbers, we need materials which are 2 numbers and wait for the product, which is their sum.

```
def plus(numA,numB):

    result = numA + numB

    return result


a = plus(2,5)

print(a)

print(type(a))
```

Output:

```
7
<type 'int'>
```

The plus() function is declared with two parameters (numA and numB) and a **return** statement. To be more detailed, the **return** statement gives us result, which equals numA + numB. When the function is called, it is assigned to a variable named *a* in the code, and the data value is stored. Because 2 and 5 are materials, the result returned from the function plus() is 7. The variable *a* is assigned to 7, so printing(a) means printing out 7. The last line is just for checking the type of *a*, which is integer. The output is exactly as expected.

How about if we use printing statement instead of the return statement?

```
def plus(numA,numB):

    result = numA + numB

    print(result)


a = plus(2,5)

print(a)

print(type(a))
```

Output:

```
7
None
<type 'NoneType'>
```

Now the function is changed slightly. The plus() prints the result instead of returning it. It means we can see the number 7 in the output, but the "product" is not actually made and the data is not stored. That's why the variable *a* does not refer to 7 as the function does not give 7 to it. Therefore, a is None and its type is NoneType.

Now the question is what if we return twice, which data values will be chosen? Does it keep the most updated one?

```
def justTest():
    print(5)
    return(6)
    print(7)
    print(8)
    return(9)

res = justTest()
print(res)
```

Output:

```
5
6
```

It is noticeable that all stuffs after the first return is not executed. 7, 8, and 9 are not printed out. This means the **return** statement terminated the execution immediately once it was executed just like the **break** keyword causes the program to exit the loop.

So can we say there is always just only one **return** statement in every function? The answer is NO!

```
def checkOdd(anum):
    if anum % 2 == 0:
        return False
    else:
        return True


print(checkOdd(5))
print(checkOdd(6))
```

Output:

```
True
False
```

The function checkOdd() is made to check if a number is an odd number or not: If the number is odd, it will return True. If not, it will return False otherwise. It can be seen that there is two **return** statements in this function, and it still works well. The **return** statement terminates the execution immediately once it was executed, but it does not mean every function just has one **return** statement.

• Better Understand Functions:

This section is designed to help you better understand and learn more how to write a function in different situations.

o When parameters are Integers:

First, let's start working with functions that made from "materials" which are Integers. For example, write a function to check if a number is a prime number or not.

```
def isPrime(anum):
    for i in range(2,anum):
        if anum % i == 0:
            return False
    return True


print(isPrime(7))
print(isPrime(8))
```

Output:

True
False

Prime numbers are just divisible by 1 and itself. Therefore, the idea to solve this problem is that if you see the number is divisible by any other number besides 1 and the number itself, it means this number is not a prime number. In this code, we check if anum can be divided by any number in the range from 2 to anum (anum is excluded). If we can find at least one, the function returns False immediately, following the idea we mentioned above. If we go through all the numbers in the for loop and still cannot find any other factor, we gets out of the loop and definitely returns True as that number is just divisible by 1 and itself.

Now, let's see how we can write a function that has more than one Integers as parameters and returns a list. For instance, write a function that returns a list of common factors of two numbers. If we put 8 and 12 in, the function is supposed to print out [1, 2, 4], and if we put 24 and 36, the output should be [1, 2, 3, 4, 6, 12]. Try it!

```python
def commonFac(numA, numB):
    result = []
    for i in range(1,numA):
        if numA % i == 0 and numB % i == 0:
            result.append(i)
    return result


print(commonFac(8,12))
print(commonFac(24,36))
```

Output:

```
[1, 2, 4]
[1, 2, 3, 4, 6, 12]
```

The output looks exactly like what we want. The rule is simple if both numA and numB can be divisible by the same number (i), that number is the common factor and added to the List result by append() method. You may question why we pick the range is from 1 to numA instead of numb. The answer is numA or numb is fine for the range. It doesn't matter if you pick numA or numB for the range because common factors are always less than these two numbers.

o When parameters are Strings

Now, let's solve problems with String parameters. Write a function to count how many times letter "a" appears in a String. For instance, "a" appears 3 times in "alibaba", 4 times in "alabama" and 0 times in "Illinois". Try it!

```
def countA(aString):
    count = 0
    for aChar in aString:
        if aChar == "a":
            count = count + 1
    return count

print(countA("alibaba"))
print(countA("alabama"))
print(countA("illinois"))
```

Output:

```
3
4
0
```

Bingo! We can count how many times "a" appears in aString given. We start at count = 0 and keep increasing by 1 whenever we see one letter "a" in the String given. After we go through all letters in that String, we exit the for loop and return the count in the end. Be careful that the return should be outside the for loop.

Now, let's do a similar problem with 2 String parameters: write a function to count how many times a given letter appears in a given String. For instance, "a" appears 3 times in "alibaba"; "e" appears 2 times in "ukulele"; and "o" appears 3 times in "colorado". Try it!

```
def countChar(aChar, aString):

    count = 0

    for item in aString:

        if item == aChar:

            count = count + 1

    return count


print(countChar("a","alibaba"))

print(countChar("e","ukulele"))

print(countChar("o","colorado"))
```

Output:

```
3
2
3
```

This problem is almost similar to the previous one. The only difference between them is the number of parameters needed for function. The idea is still the same: Going through every character in a String to see if that character matches with the character we put in parameter and count it up.

○ When parameters are Lists:

Working with functions with Strings or Integers as parameters has already helped you get familiar with making functions. Now, let's try functions with List parameters. Write a function to return a List of odd numbers in a given List of numbers. For instance, if we have a List [1, 2, 3, 4, 5], the code should print out [1, 3, 5]. Similarly, if the given material is [2, 4, 7, 8, 9], the output is supposed to be [7, 9]. Try it now!

```
def oddList(aList):

    result = []

    for aNum in aList:

        if aNum % 2 == 1:

            result.append(aNum)

    return result


print(oddList([1,2,3,4,5]))

print(oddList([2,4,7,8,9]))
```

Output:

```
[1, 3, 5]
[7, 9]
```

This is the way to go: First, we declare an empty list called result. Then, we access to every number in aList to check by using the if statement. It is noted that the remainder obtained on dividing an odd number by 2 is always 1. These odd numbers are collected and added to the List result by the append() method. Finally, when we go through all the items in aList, we exit the loop and return the result, which is a List containing all odd numbers collected.

The problem above shows us how to write a function that has a parameter that is a List. Let's try one more problem with 2 Lists put in the parameter zone. Write an intersection function that returns a List collecting elements belong to both two lists given. For instance, if two lists [1, 2, 3, 4, 5, 6] and [2, 4, 6, 8] are given, the result should be [2, 4, 6]. If the parameters are [2 , 4, 6, 8, 10] and [10, 9, 8, 7], the result should be [8, 10]. Now, try ít!

```
def intersect(listA, listB):

    result = []

    for item in listA:

        if item in listB:

            result.append(item)

    return result


print(intersect([1,2,3,4,5,6],[2,4,6,8]))

print(intersect([2,4,6,8,10],[10,9,8,7]))
```

Output:

```
[2, 4, 6]
[8, 10]
```

The logic here is simple. To begin with, we create an empty List called result. Then, we check every item in listA. If an item in listA is also in listB, we add that item to the result by the append() method. After finishing checking, we exit the loop and return the result.

▶ **Tip!**

After working with various functions in different situations, we get familiar with making a function. This is my recommendation for you to write a function:

- Determine what type of data value will be returned.
- Declare a result variable at the beginning based on the return value (not always).
- Bear in mind useful tools such as append() method.
- Be careful with local scope and variables.

• Scope of Variables:

It is important to understand scope in programming. Scope is the area in a program where a variable is declared and work. In function, variables and parameters are local. It means they work inside the area. It is called local because this variable only exists inside the function and you cannot use it outside. For example:

```
def plus(a,b):

    result = a + b

    return result


c = plus(4,5)
print(a)
```

Output:

```
builtins.NameError: name 'a' is not defined
```

When we call the function plus(4,5), that means 4 is sent to the function, and the variable a in the function now refers to 4. In the function, a is 4, but out of the function, a does not exist. Indentation and the return statement are the keys here to know what area is inside the function. That's why the output shows error name 'a' is not defined because this variable does not exist outside the function.

• Functions in Functions:

All previous functions we have written so far are called outside functions. It is interesting to know that each of the functions we write can be used and called inside other functions. This is like a big machine can be built by smaller machines which are produced from other smaller machines made from raw materials. Similarly, computer scientists take a huge problem and break it down into a group of smaller problems. Here's a simple example of a function can be used and called inside another function: Write a function to collect prime numbers in a List of numbers.

```
def isPrime(anum):
    for i in range(2,anum):
        if anum % i == 0:
            return False
    return True


def collectPrime(aList):
    result = []
    for item in aList:
        if isPrime(item) == True:
            result.append(item)
    return result

print(collectPrime([2,3,4,5,6,7,8]))
print(collectPrime([3,5,7,9,11,13,15]))
```

Output:

```
[2, 3, 5, 7]
[3, 5, 7, 11, 13]
```

It can be seen that all prime numbers from given Lists are collected and returned. Two functions are written in the code above, and one of them is used and called inside the other one. To be more detailed, the function isPrime() is called inside the function collectPrime(). We learned about the function isPrime() before, which checks if a given number is prime or not. The function collectPrime() simply checks all items in the given List. If a prime number is detected by the function isPrime(), then that number will be collected and added to the result. Finally, the result is a List of prime numbers collected and the output is exactly as expected.

✍ Check Your Understanding:

What is printed when the following statements execute?

```
def square(anum):
    result = anum * anum
    return result


def squareSum(numA, numB, numC):
    x = square(numA)
    y = square(numB)
    z = square(numC)
    return x + y + z


print(squareSum(1,2,3))
```

A) 6
B) 14
C) 36
D) Error

✓ B is the correct answer. The square() function produces the squares of numA, numb, and numC in the def squareSum(). Thanks to the square() function called inside the squareSum(), we get x = 1, y = 4, and z = 9. Therefore, the output returns 14 as 1 + 4 + 9 = 14.

• Main Function:

It can be said that the main function is where everything gets started. In Java, C++ and many other programming languages, the main function get executed first and the statements in the main function plays a crucial role in what the program does. This is not really required in Python, but it is good to have a main function to make a good structure for your code.

Because functions are designed to allow us to break up a big problem into smaller problems to tackle, it makes sense to have the main function that provide the main tasks that the program will perform. For example:

```
import math

def areaCircle(radius):
    area = math.pi * radius ** 2
    return area


def main():
    bigCircle = areaCircle(4)
    smallCircle = areaCircle(2)
    difference = bigCircle - smallCircle
    print( difference )


main()
```

Output:

```
37.6991118431
```

The result is simply the difference between areas of two circles. In Python, the word **main** is not special to function, and we actually can call this function any name we want. However, this is just all about the logic: We chose **main** because of the structure of the code and the consistency with other languages.

Before the Python interpreter executes a program, special variables are defined. _name_ is one of them and it is automatically set to the String value "__main__". When a program is imported as a module the special variable called _name_ is set to the name of the module. When a program is NOT imported, but run as the main module of a Python program, the special variable _name_ is set to the value "__main__". This means we can know whether the program is being run by itself or whether it is being used by other programs. Due to this, we can decide to choose to execute the code we have written or not.

```python
def plus(a,b):

    return a + b


def multiple(a,b):

    return a * b


def main():

    numA = int(input("Please enter the first number"))

    numB = int(input("Please enter the second number"))

    print(plus(numA,numB))

    print(multiple(numA,numB))

if __name__ == "__main__":

    main()
```

Output:

```
9
20
```

This is the output when we put 4 and 5 as parameters for the function called. It is noticeable that instead of just calling the main() function, the statement if __name__ == "__main__" is used to ask what the value of the __name__ variable is. If the value is "__main__", then the main function will be called. If not, it is assumed that the program is imported into another program and we do not want to call main because that program will invoke the functions as needed.

Conditional statement to execute our main function is useful in case we are writing code that may be used by others. To execute the main function conditionally, we used an if statement to create a selection.

We have covered lots of stuffs and gain much knowledge about Function. Now it's time to practice as writing a function needs a lot of practice.

🐰 Chapter Review Questions:

1. Write a function called triMulti to multiply 3 numbers. For instance, triMulti(2,3,4) would return 24 since 2 * 3 * 4 = 24, and triMulti(1,2,3) would return 6 as 1 * 2 * 3 = 6.

2. Write a function called isPositive that returns True if a number is positive and False if it is not.

3. Write a function called factorList to return list of factors of a number. For instance, factorList(15) would return [1,3,5,15], and factorList(12) would return [1,2,3,4,6,12].

4. Write a function called sumFactor to return the sum of all factors of a number. For instance, sumFactor(6) would return 12 because 1 +2 +3 +6 = 12.

5. Write a function called commonFac to return list of common factors of 2 numbers. For instance, commonFac(36,24) would return [1,2,3,4,6,12], and commonFac(12,18) would return [1,2,3,6].

6. Write a function called gcf to return the greatest common factor of 2 numbers. For instance, gcf(36,24) would return 12.

7. Write a function called primeFactor to return list of factors that are prime numbers. For instance, primeFactor(196) would return [2,7], and primeFactor(13195) would return [5,7,13,29].

8. Write a function called checkChar that returns True if a character is in that String and False if it is not. For instance, checkChar("a", "alibaba") would return True, but checkChar("o","luther") would return False.

9. Write a function called posChar to return positions of a character in a String given. For instance, posChar("a","alibaba") would return [0,4,6], and posChar("i", "mississippi") would return [1,4,7,10].

10. Write a function called reverseString that reverse a given String. For instance, reverseString("hello") would return "olleh", and reverseString("never again") would return "niaga reven".

11. Write a function called isPalindrome that returns True if a given String is a palindrome and False if it is not. A palindrome is a String that have characters read the same backward as forward. For example, "hannah", "radar", "anna" and "mom" are all palindromes.

12. Write a function called moreA that return the String that has more letter "a" between two Strings given. For instance, moreA("alibaba", "alabama") would return "alabama" because "alabama" has 4 letters "a", while "alibaba" just has 3 letters "a". If they have the same number of letter "a", the function should return None.

13. Write a function called countOdd that returns the number of odd numbers in a List given. For instance, countOdd([1,2,3,4,6]) would return 2, and countOdd([34,12,67,24,86,13,77]) would return 3.

14. Write a function called oddList that return odd numbers in a List given. For instance, oddList([1,2,3,4,5]) would return [1,3,5], and oddList([2,4,6,8,9,7] would return [9,7].

15. Write a function called sumList that returns the sum of all numbers in a List given. For instance, sumList([1,2,3,4,5]) would return 15, and sumList([5,10,15,20,25]) would return 75.

16. Write a function called maxNum that return the greatest number in a List of numbers given. For instance, maxNum([2,6,1,7,3]) would return 7, and maxNum([23,62,2,56,21]) would return 62.

17. Write a function called delDup that return a new List that all duplicates in the old List are removed. For instance, delDup([4,1,2,1,4,3]) would return [4,1,2,3], and delDup(["a", "b", "s", "b", "g", "a"]) would return ["a", "b", "s", "g"]).

18. Write a function called primeList that return prime numbers in a List given. For instance, primeList([11,12,13,14,15]) would return [11,13], and primeList([2,25,31,42,47]) would return [2,31,47].

19. Write a function called intersect that return a List containing elements exist in both Lists given. For instance, intersect([1,2,3,4], [1,3]) would return [1,3]), and intersect([3,7,5,8,2], [5,2,4,8,1]) would return [5, 8, 2].

20.* Write a function called mySort() to return a List sorted from a List given. For instance, mySort([4,2,7,1,3,6]) would return [1,2,3,4,6,7].

▶ All the solutions are on the next page. Try your best to solve all of these problems before checking the answers.

(*) The last question is the hard one.

✓ Solutions:

1) Solution to Question 1:

```
def triMulti(a,b,c):

  return a * b * c


print(triMulti(1,2,3))

print(triMulti(2,3,4))
```

2) Solution to Question 2:

```
def isPositive(anum):

  if anum > 0 :

    return True

  else:

    return False


print(isPositive(5))

print(isPositive(-2))
```

3) Solution to Question 3:

```
def factorList(anum):

  result = []

  for i in range(1,anum+1):

    if anum % i == 0:

      result.append(i)

  return result
```

```
print(factorList(12))

print(factorList(15))
```

4) Solution to Question 4:

```
def sumFactor(anum):
    result = 0
    for i in range(1,anum+1):
      if anum % i == 0:
         result = result + i
    return result

print(sumFactor(6))
print(sumFactor(12))
```

5) Solution to Question 5:

```
def commonFac(numA, numB):
    result = []
    for i in range (1,numA):
      if numA % i == 0 and numB % i == 0:
         result.append(i)
    return result

print(commonFac(36,24))
print(commonFac(12,18))
```

6) Solution to Question 6:

```
def gcf(numA, numB):
    result = []
    for i in range (1,numA):
        if numA % i == 0 and numB % i == 0:
            result.append(i)
    return result[-1]


print(gcf(36,24))
print(gcf(12,18))
```

7) Solution to Question 7:

```
def isPrime(a):
    for i in range(2,a):
        if a % i == 0:
            return False
    return True


def primeFactor(anum):
    result = []
    for i in range(2,anum+1):
        if anum % i == 0 and isPrime(i) == True:
            result.append(i)
    return result


print(primeFactor(196))
print(primeFactor(13195))
```

8) Solution to Question 8:

```python
def checkChar(achar,aString):
    if achar in aString:
        return True
    else:
        return False


print(checkChar("a","alibaba"))
print(checkChar("o","luther"))
```

9) Solution to Question 9:

```python
def posChar(achar,aString):
    result = []
    for i in range(len(aString)):
        if achar == aString[i]:
            result.append(i)
    return result


print(posChar("a","alibaba"))
print(posChar("i", "mississippi"))
```

10) Solution to Question 10:

```python
def reverseString(aString):
    result = ""
    for i in range(len(aString)):
```

```
        result = aString[i] + result

    return result


print(reverseString("hello"))

print(reverseString("never again"))
```

11) Solution to Question 11:

```
def isPalindrome(aString):

    for i in range(len(aString)):

        if aString[i] != aString[len(aString)-1-i]:

            return False

    return True


print(isPalindrome("hannah"))

print(isPalindrome("hannoh"))
```

12) Solution to Question 12:

```
def countA(aString):

    result = 0

    for achar in aString:

        if achar == "a":

            result = result + 1

    return result


def moreA(stringA,stringB):

    if countA(stringA) > countA(stringB):
```

```
    return stringA

  elif countA(stringA) < countA(stringB):

    return stringB

  else:

    return None


print(moreA("alibaba","alabama"))

print(moreA("alaska","panama"))
```

13) Solution to Question 13:

```
def countOdd(alist):

  count = 0

  for item in alist:

    if item % 2 == 1:

      count = count + 1

  return count


print(countOdd([1,2,3,4,6]))

print(countOdd([34,12,67,24,86,13,77]))
```

14) Solution to Question 14:

```
def oddList(alist):

  result = []

  for item in alist:

    if item % 2 == 1:

      result.append(item)
```

```
    return result

print(oddList([1,2,3,4,5]))

print(oddList([2,4,6,8,9,7]))
```

15) Solution to Question 15:

```
def sumList(alist):
    result = 0
    for item in alist:
        result = result + item
    return result

print(sumList([1,2,3,4,5]))
print(sumList([5,10,15,20,25]))
```

16) Solution to Question 16:

```
def maxNum(alist):
    result = alist[0]
    for item in alist:
        if item > result:
            result = item
    return result

print(maxNum([2,6,1,7,3]))
print(maxNum([23,62,2,56,21]))
```

17) Solution to Question 17:

```
def delDup(alist):
    result = []
    for item in alist:
        if item not in result:
            result.append(item)
    return result


print(delDup([4,1,2,1,4,3]))
print(delDup(["a", "b", "s", "b", "g", "a"]))
```

18) Solution to Question 18:

```
def isPrime(anum):
    for i in range(2,anum):
        if anum % i == 0:
            return False
    return True


def primeList(alist):
    result = []
    for item in alist:
        if isPrime(item) == True:
            result.append(item)
    return result


print(primeList([11,12,13,14,15]))
print(primeList([2,25,31,42,47]))
```

19) Solution to Question 19:

```
def intersect(listA,listB):
    result = []
    for item in listA:
        if item in listB:
            result.append(item)
    return result

print(intersect([1,2,3,4],[1,3]))
print(intersect([3,7,5,8,2],[5,2,4,8,1]))
```

20) Solution to Question 20:

```
def mySort(aList):
    for i in range(len(aList)):
        minIndex = i
        for j in range(i + 1,len(aList)):
            if aList[j] < aList[minIndex]:
                minIndex = j
        temp = aList[minIndex]
        aList[minIndex] = aList[i]
        aList[i] = temp

myList=[4,2,7,1,3,6]
mySort(myList)
print(myList)
```

CHAPTER 9: FILES

So far we have learned coding with the data already in the program as well as received from the input by user. However, in some situations, getting users to enter data may not be practical if our program need a huge amount of data such as student information. In real life, most of data are from files. In chapter 9, we will go through Python concepts to use and handle data from files in our programs.

• Opening & Reading Files:

One of the most fundamentals to handle files is reading from a file given. In this section, we are going to learn how to read from a simple text file. Supposed we have a text file called student.txt with the following lines:

Names Scores

michael 80 85 70 90 70

steve 83 86 79 92 75

mary 82 87 74 82 97

sucre 92 68 71 95 76

john 84 72 85 86 89

This is how the text file looks like:

Save that text file and your Python file at the same place. It can be at the desktop or a local disk as long as they are at the same place. Now try this code:

```
myfile = open("student.txt","r")


line1 = myfile.readline()

line2 = myfile.readline()

print(line1)

print(line2)


myfile.close()
```

Output:

```
Names Scores

michael 80 85 70 90 70
```

In Python, we have to open files before we can use them and close files when we are done. The first line of the code above opens the text file given with the statement open("student.txt","r") and refers it to the variable named *myfile*. After going through the whole data, the code ends by closing the file with the statement myfile.close(). It is noted that we put two things inside the parentheses: The first one is the file name "student.txt", and the other one is "r", which stands for our purpose of opening the file: "read". Next, myfile.readline() simply reads every line in the file, so it reads the first line for the first time and then reads the next line for the second time we call it. Thus, the output is exactly what we expected: the first two lines are printed.

It is noted that if you do not save the file used and your code in the same folder, you need to provide the actual path where you stored the text file. For example, if you store student.txt in a folder named PythonProjects on your drive C, you should put "C:\\PythonProjects\\student.txt".

Is there any way to read every line in a file given more efficiently than just using readline() to read only one line as we did with the previous example? The answer is Yes! Use the for loop!

```python
myfile = open("student.txt","r")

for aline in myfile:

    print(aline)

myfile.close()
```

Output:

```
Names Scores

michael 80 85 70 90 70

steve 83 86 79 92 75

mary 82 87 74 82 97

sucre 92 68 71 95 76

john 84 72 85 86 89
```

The for loop goes through the text file line by line, so the variable *aline* declared in the for loop exactly refers to a line in the file. This is an efficient way to access to all the lines in the file instead of using the readline() statements 6 times in this case.

Besides the for loop, the while loop can also be used to do this stuff:

```python
myfile = open("student.txt", "r")

aline = myfile.readline()

while aline:

    print(aline)

    aline = myfile.readline()

myfile.close()
```

Output:

Names Scores
michael 80 85 70 90 70
steve 83 86 79 92 75
mary 82 87 74 82 97
sucre 92 68 71 95 76
john 84 72 85 86 89

It makes sense as aline=myfile.readline() statement reads the first line at the first time it is called, so it is good to make a starting point here. After that the while loop helps us go through all lines in the file as while aline means the process keeps going until there is no aline anymore. The increment to make sure it keeps going to the next line is the statement on line 5. Finally, we close the file as usual.

• Writing To Files:

The job of data processing tasks is usually reading data from a file, manipulating it by some ways, and then writing data to a new file for some particular purposes. So far we have discussed the opening and reading parts, which help us create a new file ready for writing. Remember it was said we put the letter "r" inside the parentheses when opening our file, which stands for our purpose of opening the file: "read". How about if our purpose now is "write"? The letter "w", similarly, should stands for it.

When we open a file for writing, a new and empty file is created to receive our data. The write method takes one parameter, a String and enables us to put data into a text file. Before trying writing some data to a file, try printing out just names of students in student.txt by this code:

```
infile = open("student.txt", "r")

aline = infile.readline()

while aline:

    items = aline.split()

    name = items[0]

    print(name)

    aline = infile.readline()


infile.close()
```

Output:

Names
michael
steve
mary
sucre
john

From the code above, items refers to the List containing every elements separated by white spaces in a line. Names are all the first element of every line, so items[0] is the name of students in the text file. Therefore, all names are printed out as expected.

Now, let's think about a situation: we are given a data file and supposed to write back an expected output. This is a very common scene in programming. In this case, we are given a text file storing names of students and their grades. How about if our job is to give back another file that just contains names of students?

```
infile = open("student.txt", "r")

outfile = open("studentnames.txt", "w")


aline = infile.readline()

while aline:

    items = aline.split()

    name = items[0]

    outfile.write(name + '\n')

    aline = infile.readline()


infile.close()

outfile.close()
```

Output:

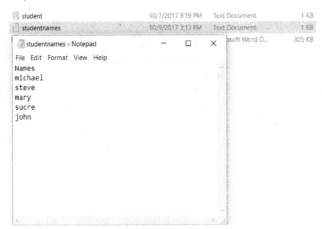

When the code above gets executed, a text file called studentnames.txt is created with all data is written into. Instead of just printing out as the previous example does, this code created a new text file and put the output into it. The *infile*

variable is for opening the file to read, while the *outfile* is the where we create and put the data in. This syntax '\n' allows us to go to the next line. That's why names of all students are printed in every single line instead of just only 1 line.

Now, the question is can we write data directly to the file we are opening instead of creating a new file? The answer is Yes.

To do that, we'll use the "a" mode, which stands for "append" instead of "w" mode. Our purpose now is not writing to a new file but appending new stuffs to an old file. This is how we do it:

```
myfile = open("student.txt","a")

myfile.write("This is the first thing I write")

myfile.write("This is the second")

myfile.close()
```

Output:

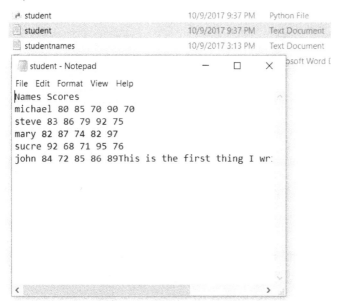

Oops! It looks like the code starts writing data right next to last character in the text file, not from the new line as we think. This is not a big deal as we can fix it with the "\n" technique. Trying printing this mistake on purpose helps you see where it will start more clearly, so you can append stuffs to the old file more efficiently. This is how we fix it:

```
myfile = open("student.txt","a")

myfile.write("\nThis is the first thing I write")

myfile.write("\nThis is the second")

myfile.close()
```

Output:

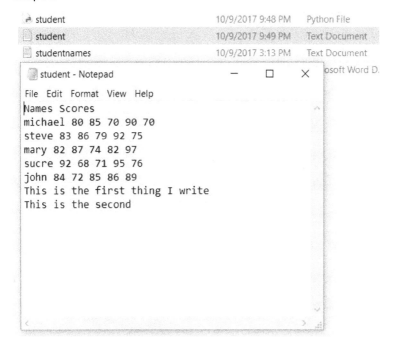

Here we go! Everything is printed smoothly because of the "\n" syntax and because of the previous example which helps us know exactly from where the data is added to the old file.

• File Handling Review and More:

Supposed we have a file variable called myfile, and filename stands for any file such as "student.txt" or "studentnames.txt".

Method	Statement	Explanation
open	open(filename, "r")	This opens the file given and use it for reading purpose. It returns a reference to a file object.
open	open(filename, "w")	This opens the file given and use it for writing purpose. It returns a reference to a file object.
open	open(filename, "a")	This opens the file given and use it for append purpose. It returns a reference to a file object.
close	myfile.close()	This closes the file to complete process.
read	myfile.read()	Reads and return the entire file as a single String.
read(n)	myfile.read(n)	Reads and return a String of n characters.
readline()	myfile.readline()	Reads one entire line from the file. A trailing newline character is kept in the string.
readline(n)	myfile.readline(n)	Return n characters if the line is longer than n.
readlines()	myfile.readlines()	Return a list of Strings and each of them represents a single line of the file.
readlines(n)	myfile.readlines(n)	Read and return n characters. An entire line is returned because n is rounded up.
write	myfile.write(aString)	Add aString to the end of the file, and myfile refers to a file that has been opened and used for writing purpose.
writeline()	myfile.writeline(sequence)	Writes a sequence of Strings to the file. The sequence can be any iterable object producing Strings, typically a List of Strings.

📓 Chapter Review Questions:

Given this text file called student.txt, complete questions below:

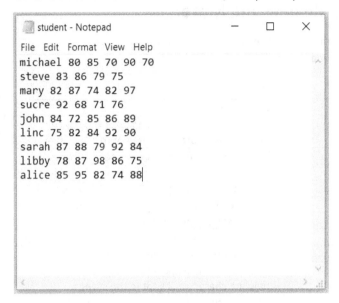

1) Using the text file "student.txt" write a code that prints out the names of students that missed quiz test. To be more specific, every student is supposed to have 5 quiz grades, so who don't have enough 5 quiz grades are students that missed quiz test.

2) Using the text file "student.txt" write a code that calculates the average grade for each student (students who missed the quiz test are forgiven, so it doesn't matter if they don't have enough 5 test grades).

3) Using the text file "student.txt" write a code that prints out the names of students that have never ever scored over 90 in the test.

4) Using the text file "student.txt" write a code to find the minimum and maximum scores for each student. Print out their name to see it more clearly.

5) Using the text file "student.txt" write a code to write a new text file that rank students based on their average scores.

Solutions:

1)

```
myfile = open("student.txt","r")

for aline in myfile:
    if len(aline.split()) < 6:
        print(aline)

myfile.close()
```

2)

```
myfile = open("student.txt","r")

for aline in myfile:
    name = aline.split()[0]
    scores = aline.split()[1:]
    sumscores = 0
    for aScore in scores:
        sumscores = sumscores + int(aScore)
    averageScore = sumscores / len(scores)
    print(name, averageScore)

myfile.close()
```

3)

```
myfile = open("student.txt","r")


for aline in myfile:

    name = aline.split()[0]

    scores = aline.split()[1:]

    found = True

    for aScore in scores:

        if int(aScore) >= 90:

            found = False

    if found:

        print(name, scores)


myfile.close()
```

4)

```
myfile = open("student.txt", "r")


for aline in myfile:

    name = aline.split()[0]

    scores = aline.split()[1:]

    print(name, "max is", max(scores), "min is", min(scores))


myfile.close()
```

5)

```
myfile = open("student.txt","r")

outfile = open("ranking.txt", "w")

scoreBoard = {}

for aline in myfile:

    name = aline.split()[0]

    scores = aline.split()[1:]

    sumscores = 0

    for aScore in scores:

        sumscores = sumscores + int(aScore)

    averageScore = sumscores / len(scores)

    scoreBoard[name] = averageScore

sortedScores = [(k,v) for v,k in sorted([(v,k) for k,v in scoreBoard.items()], reverse=True)]

for item in sortedScores:

    outfile.write(item[0] + " " + str(item[1]) + '\n')

myfile.close()

outfile.close()
```

ranking   10/10/2017 11:19 ..   Text Document

ranking - Notepad   — □ ×

File Edit Format View Help
```
sarah 86.0
libby 84.8
alice 84.8
linc 84.6
mary 84.4
john 83.2
steve 80.75
michael 79.0
sucre 76.75
```

❖ Coding Challenge:

Supposed we have a text file "story.txt", write a code to write a new text file called "wordsStat.txt" that collects every different word used in the story, the number of times that word appears in the text, and lines that contain that word.

The story.txt file should look like this:

It is not necessary to use exactly that file. You can create your own story.txt file by copying a short story somewhere. The main purpose of this exercise is improving your file handling skills by collecting different words, counting how many times a word appears and tracking lines that contain that word. Good news for you is that you don't need to sort words, it can be placed unorderly. Your output should be like this:

```
wordStats - Notepad
File  Edit  Format  View  Help
'one' appears 1 times in lines [1]

'fine' appears 3 times in lines [1, 3, 9]

'evening' appears 1 times in lines [1]

'a' appears 21 times in lines [1, 3, 5, 15, 21, 23, 33, 62, 64, 68, 70]

'young' appears 4 times in lines [1, 17, 42, 68]

'princess' appears 19 times in lines [1, 3, 11, 17, 19, 23, 25, 30, 37, 42, 43, 45,

'put' appears 5 times in lines [1, 5, 15, 49]

'on' appears 7 times in lines [1, 3, 9, 15, 43, 62]

'her' appears 19 times in lines [1, 3, 17, 19, 30, 32, 49, 62, 64]

'bonnet' appears 1 times in lines [1]

'and' appears 59 times in lines [1, 3, 5, 9, 11, 15, 17, 19, 23, 27, 30, 33, 35, 39,

'clogs' appears 1 times in lines [1]

'went' appears 2 times in lines [1, 51]

'out' appears 10 times in lines [1, 5, 11, 23, 33, 47, 51, 64, 70]
```

✓ Solutions:

```python
import re

myfile = open("story.txt", "r")

outfile = open("wordStats.txt", "w")

wordlist = []

countlist = []

listoflines = []

lineNum = 0

for aline in myfile:

    lineNum = lineNum + 1

    wordline = re.sub("[^a-zA-Z]"," ", aline)

    linelist = wordline.split()

    for aword in linelist:

        if aword.lower() not in wordlist:

            wordlist.append(aword.lower())

            countlist.append(1)

            listoflines.append([lineNum])

        else:

            countlist[wordlist.index(aword.lower())] += 1

            listoflines[wordlist.index(aword.lower())].append(lineNum)

def removeDup(alist):

    result = []

    for item in alist:

        if item not in result:

            result.append(item)

    return result

for i in range(len(wordlist)):

    outfile.write("\n" + "'" + wordlist[i] + "'" + " appears " + str(countlist[i]) + " times in lines " +
str(removeDup(listoflines[i])) + "\n")

myfile.close()

outfile.close()
```

CHAPTER 10: CLASS

• Object-Oriented Programming & Classes:

Object-oriented programming is an approach to programming that breaks a huge and complicated problems into smaller objects that interact with each other. Python is an object-oriented programming language. This means we can use objects and define our own classes of objects with Python.

In object-oriented programming, the focus is on the creation of objects which contain both data and functionality together. Objects are created from templates known as classes. A class can be considered as a type which can be *int, str, bool,* or other types we have learned so far. In other words, we can say that classes provide definitions for objects. For example, The int class defines what Integers are and how they work in Python.

• Create Your Own Class:

We start creating our own class by using the **class** keyword followed by the name of the class. Now, let's try creating an Vertex class for the first example. Defining an Vertex class hasn't actually created an Vertex. Instead, what we've created here is a sort of instruction manual or a blueprint for constructing "Vertex" objects.

```
class Vertex:
    def __init__(self):
        self.x = 0
        self.y = 0


vertexA = Vertex()
print(vertexA)
```

Output:

<__main__.Vertex object at 0x03407250>

The output shows that vertexA is a Vertex object, which is a new type that we created by defining a new class called Vertex. Classes can be created anywhere in a program, but they are usually placed at the beginning. The class definition begins with the keyword **class** followed by the name of the class, and ends with a colon.

Noticeably, this is the first time you have seen a special name **__init__** in the code, and every class should have it. This is known as the initializer or the constructor of the class. We cannot name it anything we want. It is always named **init** with two underscores on the left and right sides. All special methods have two underscores around their names, and Python have many special methods besides **__init__**. An initializer method is automatically called whenever an object of the class is created. In this case, this initializer is called whenever a new instance of Vertex is created. I know you are still not familiar with it as this is new and different from all of what we learned before.

It is noted that in the process of initialization, we created two variable names called x and y, and gave them both equal 0. Although nothing shows in the output, vertexA in this code actually has been created, having an x and y coordinate with value 0. In other words, vertexA is the vertex (0,0) just like the point (0,0) in Maths.

Besides, we need to add **self** in front of these variable names. The **self** keyword refers to an instance itself. The **self** parameter is automatically set to reference the newly created object that needs to be initialized. This keyword seems confusing at this point but you will get more familiar and understand it through examples and projects.

So far, we have learned to write our constructor that create a vertex at location (0,0). To create more vertices at different positions, we have to build a constructor with parameters that allows the user to pass specific information to the constructor. We can make our class constructor more flexible by putting extra parameters into the __init__ method. For example:

```
class Vertex:

    def __init__(self, valX, valY):
        self.x = valX
        self.y = valY

vertexA = Vertex(2,5)

print(vertexA)
```

Output:

```
<__main__.Vertex object at 0x03479190>
```

Similar to the previous example, the output gain shows that vertexA is a Vertex object. However, the difference is that vertexA now is no longer (0, 0). Now when we create new vertices, we can provide the details of x and y coordinates through parameters. When the point is created, the values of valX and valY are assigned to the state of the object.

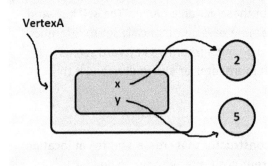

• Class Methods:

We already had a class called Vertex as well as built its constructor, which can be used to store all relevant data of a vertex object. Within this class, we can declare two variables to store the x and y coordinates of a point. Additionally, we can add methods to the Vertex class to support operations for vertices. In this example, we will add two methods call getX() and getY(), which help us get the value of x and y coordinates.

```
class Vertex:
    def __init__(self, valX, valY):
        self.x = valX
        self.y = valY
    def getX(self):
        return self.x
    def getY(self):
        return self.y


vertexA = Vertex(2,5)
print(vertexA.getX())
print(vertexA.getY())
```

Output:

```
2
5
```

Now we can see a clear output. The methods getX() and getY() return the value of x and y coordinates of the vertex object. Therefore, 2 and 5 are printed out as 2 is the value of x coordinate, and 5 is the value of y coordinate. To be more detailed, you can see from the code above that the getX() method simply returns self.x from the object itself. Interstingly, the class constructor clearly stated that self.x equals valX, and valX is a parameter of vertex objects when they are created. When we created Vertex(2,5), it means valX is 2 and so is self.x also refers to 2. Therefore, it returns 2 as the method returns self.x. Likewise, the getY() method looks the same.

You'll notice that a method behaves like a function but it is invoked on a specific instance. Also, unlike functions, a method exists inside the class and most methods have **self** as their parameters. Why do methods defined in a class have **self** as their parameter? This is because it serves as reference to the object itself which in turn gives access to the state data inside the object. In this case, these two simple methods allow vertexA to give us its state incoordination. The getX method returns the value of the x coordinate, while the getY returns the value of the y coordinate.

• String Method:

This is a very interesting method. The String method, written as __str__, can be understood as an "appearance" of an object created. Remember when we try to print out vertexA, the output just lets us know that it is a Vertex object without showing any information about its coordinates. The String method can improve this "appearance" by making the objects readable as well as showing clearly the state of the Vertex in this situation.

This method is also a special method as __init__, so the syntax is still similar with two underscores on both sides of the name. The __str__ method creates and returns a string which is a representation as defined by the class creator, and you can code to decide how it should look like when it is printed out. For example:

```
class Vertex:

    def __init__(self, valX, valY):

        self.x = valX

        self.y = valY

    def getX(self):

        return self.x

    def getY(self):

        return self.y

    def __str__(self):

        return "(" + str(self.x) + ", " + str(self.y) + ")"


vertexA = Vertex(2,5)

print(vertexA)
```

Output:

```
(2, 5)
```

Bingo! Now the output looks exactly like what a point is represented in Math. This is what we expected to see a Vertex. Also, as I said before, you can code to decide how it should look like when it is printed out. So if I change the __str__ method to this one below, the output will be different:

```
    def __str__(self):

        return "x=" + str(self.x) + ", y=" + str(self.y)
```

Output:

x=2, y=5

Now the output does not show the Vertex the way it appears in Math, but it also gives information of the Vertex by showing its x and y coordinates.

What happened if we get rid of the __str__ method? You saw it before! The ouput would be like this:

<__main__.Vertex object at 0x03479190>

To re capitulate, the __str__() takes one parameter self and should return a String. If you don't return something at the end of your __str__(), Python will get confused, throw an error, and your program will stop running.

Some may ask why do we still have to write a printing method instead of just using print statement as before? The reason is that default implementations provided by Python do not do exactly what we want as you saw it, and we programmers can change it. When we change the meaning of a special method, it means we override the method.

• Use Objects as Arguments:

After creating objects and some methods to operate them, now let's use these objects for another role – playing as arguments. In this section, we will learn how to pass an object as an argument in the usual way. We are going to write a simple function called slopeCal involving our new Point objects. The job of this function is to calculate the slope of the line made by two points.

Remember in Math: given two points A and B, the line passing through both of these points is AB, and the slope of this line is calculated by the formula:

Slope of AB = $(y_B - y_A) / (x_B - x_A)$

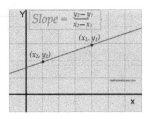

```
class Vertex:
    def __init__(self, valX, valY):
        self.x = valX
        self.y = valY
    def getX(self):
        return self.x
    def getY(self):
        return self.y
    def __str__(self):
        return "(" + str(self.x) + ", " + str(self.y) + ")"


def slopeCal(vertex1, vertex2):
    differY = vertex2.getY() - vertex1.getY()
    differX = vertex2.getX() - vertex1.getX()
    if differX == 0 :
        return "undefined"
    else:
        slope = differY / differX
        return slope


vertexA = Vertex(2,5)
vertexB = Vertex(3,1)
print(slopeCal(vertexA,vertexB))
```

Output:

-4.0

According to the Math formula, the slope of the line passing through vertexA (2, 5) and vertex (3,1) is supposed to be (1 – 5) / (3 – 2), which equals to -4.0. Thus, the output is as expected. The if statement is used to make sure that if two points have the same x values, the slope is undefined.

• Return Instances:

As we know, functions as well as methods return values, and everything in Python is an object. Therefore, it makes sense to say that functions and methods can also return objects. For example, we learned that functions return Integers, Strings or Lists, which are actually Python objects, so Vertex should be returnable as it is an object we created. The slightly difference here is that we want to have a method that creates an object using the constructor and then return it as the value of the method.

To test this, we is going to try a method called symmetryPoint() that return the Vertex which is symmetrical to a given vertex via the origin (0,0) . For example, the vertex H(3, 2) will have the symmetryPoint K(-3, -2) as shown below. Therefore, if we have vertexA(2, 5), the method is supposed to return the vertex that has coordinates (-2, -5).

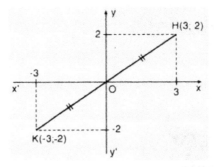

```python
class Vertex:

    def __init__(self, valX, valY):
        self.x = valX
        self.y = valY

    def getX(self):
        return self.x

    def getY(self):
        return self.y

    def __str__(self):
        return "(" + str(self.x) + ", " + str(self.y) + ")"

    def symmetryPoint(self, aVertex):
        newX = - (self.x)
        newY = - (self.y)
        return Vertex(newX, newY)

vertexA = Vertex(2,5)
symmetryA = vertexA.symmetryPoint(vertexA)
print(symmetryA)
```

Output:

```
(-2, -5)
```

The resulting Vertex, symmetryA, has an x value of -2 and a y value of -5, and it is represented as (-2, -5). This is exactly what we expect to see from the output.

• Python Special Methods:

We knew that Python comes with many special methods. These methods are also known as magic methods and are always surrounded by double underscores. Two of the magic methods that we have discovered so far are __init__ and __str__.

One of the interesting things of a special method is that we do not invoke it directly. For example, when we want to call and use the __str__ method, we CANNOT write:

vertexA.__str__()

Instead, we write:

print(vertexA)

I know this is very strange, but this is why we call it "magic" method and how it works. One more thing about special methods is that we can override them to make them work the way we want. Besides __init__ and __str__ methods, which other special methods that we need to know?

There are actually a lot of Python magic methods that you can explore more and check it on this link: https://docs.python.org/3/reference/datamodel.html. However, in this book, we will not go through all of them. Instead, some of them chosen in this section are enough to help you understand more how magic methods work and get more familiar with them.

Suppose x is an instance of a class that implements these methods; y is the parameter passed in to work with x; seq stands for sequence; key and value are simply as keys and values of Dictionary we learned before. The table below review some fundamental magic methods and how they work:

Magic Methods	Description	How You Write It
__init__()	to initialize an instance	x = ClassName()
__str__()	make objects readable	repr(x)
__repr__()	official representation as a String	str(x)
__iter__()	to iterate through a sequence	iter(seq)
__next__()	to get the next value from iterator	next(seq)
__len__()	the number of items	len(seq)
__contains__(x)	to know whether it contains a value	x in seq
__getitem__(key)	to get a value by its key	x[key]
__setitem__(key,value)	to set a value by its key	x[key] = value
__delitem__(key)	to delete a key-value pair	del x[key]
__add__(y)	addition	x + y
__sub__(y)	subtraction	x − y
__mul__(y)	multiplication	x * y
__truediv__(y)	division	x / y
__mod__(y)	modulo (remainder)	x % y
__pow__(y)	power	x ** y
__lshift__(y)	shift left	x << y
__rshift__(y)	shift right	x >> y
__and__(y)	and relation	x & y
__or__(y)	or relation	x ^ y
__eq__(y)	equality	x == y
__gt__(y)	greater than y	x > y
__ge__(y)	greater than or equal to y	x >= y
__lt__(y)	less than y	x < y
__le__(y)	less than or equal to y	x <= y
__new__()	a class constructor	x = ClassName()
__del__()	a class destructor	del(x)
__hash__()	hash values given	hash(x)

Let's use some of them from the table above to write a complete program and see how they work. This will help you have more ideas about magic methods and understand how they work in an object-oriented program.

• A Complete Object-Oriented Program:

Now, it's time to write a program called Fraction that contains some magic methods as we promised last section. 5 methods are chosen from the table to create this class are __init__, __str__, __eq__, __add__, and __mul__.

```python
class Fraction:
    def __init__(self, numerator, denominator):
        self.num = numerator
        self.den = denominator
    def __str__(self):
        return str(self.num) + "/" + str(self.den)
    def __eq__(self, other):
        if self.num * other.den == self.den * other.num:
            return True
        else:
            return False
    def __add__(self, other):
        newDen = self.den * other.den
        newNum = self.num * other.den + other.num * self.den
        return Fraction(newNum, newDen)
    def __mul__(self, other):
        return Fraction(self.num * other.num, self.den * other.den)

a = Fraction(1,2)
b = Fraction(2,3)
```

```
print(a)

print(a == b)

print(a + b)

print(a*b)
```

Output:

```
1/2
False
7/6
2/6
```

Firstly, the constructor __init__ is created to gets the information it needs from the user, storing data values for numerator and denominator of a Fraction.

Secondly, a is declared to be equal to Fraction(1,2), and the __str__() method helps it to be printed out with a readable form. Therefore, Fraction(1,2) is demonstrated as 1/2, which is very similar to what we know and learn in Math. Again, we can see the power of writing a __str__ in the Class creation.

Thirdly, thanks to the __eq__ method, a == b returns False since 1/2 is not equal to 2/3. You may ask why we have to write __eq__ because Python has to know how to compare values. Noticeably, if we just normally compare 1/2 and 2/3, Python might help us evaluate this comparison. However, the comparison between Fraction(1,2) and Fraction(2,3) is confusing to Python because they are our own objects. Therefore, __eq__ is written to compare two values the way we want. In this case, I applied the cross-multiply rule in Math to compare two Fractions. 1/2 is not equal to 2/3, so it returns False

Fourthly, __add__ is written to evaluate if we want to add two Fraction objects. It means whenever a + b needs to be calculated and a and b are Fractions objects, the __add__ method written in the class Fraction will be called and used. The logic is still the same as it is in Math:

$$\frac{1}{2} + \frac{2}{3} = \frac{1 \times 3}{2 \times 3} + \frac{2 \times 2}{3 \times 2} = \frac{3}{6} + \frac{4}{6} = \frac{7}{6}$$

The denominator of the result is basically the multiplication of two denominators given, while the numerator of the result is the sum of the product of the first numerator and the second denominator and the product of the second numerator and the first denominator.

Fifthly, __mul__ evaluates the multiplication of two objects. It has simpler rule as we just need to multiply two numerators to get the new numerators and two denominators to get the new denominators.

$$\frac{1}{2} \times \frac{2}{3} = \frac{1 \times 2}{2 \times 3} = \frac{2}{6}$$

It is noted that the ways that all of these methods are called are interesting. Instead of writing a.__eq__(b), a.__add__(b), or a.__mul__(b), they are automatically called and used when we just write a == b, a + b, or a * b.

If you wish to simplify the result $\frac{2}{6} = \frac{1}{3}$, you can write a simplify() function to take care of this job as well as import or write a gcd() funtion, which stands for greatest common divisor, to support your simplify() function. Challenge yourself by doing it by yourself!

• Inheritance:

Inheritance is one of the key concepts of object-oriented programming, and Python supports inheritance. Inheritance allows us to create a new class from an existing class so that we can reuse existing code. A class can inherit attributes and behavior methods from another class, which is called the superclass as well as ancestors. A class which inherits from a superclass is called a subclass or child class.

► Syntax for Inheritance:

```
class SuperClass:

    #Code for of superclass

class SubClass(BaseClass):

    #Code for subclass
```

Let's write a superclass called Employee and its subclass called Engineer for example. Because our plan is the class Engineer is going to be the subclass of the class Employee, we put "Employee" inside the parentheses at the class Engineer creation, following the structure described above.

```
class Employee:

    def __init__(self, firstname, lastname, age, pay):

        self.firstname = firstname

        self.lastname = lastname

        self.age = age

        self.pay = pay

        self.email = firstname + "." + lastname + "@techcomp.com"

    def __str__(self):

        return str(self.firstname) + " " + str(self.lastname) + "(age: " + str(self.age) + ")"

    def calculatePay(self):

        hours = input("Enter the number of hours: ")

        hourlyRate = input("Enter the hourly rate: ")

        self.pay = int(hours) * int(hourlyRate)

        return self.pay


class Engineer(Employee):

    pass
```

```
a = Employee("Lam", "Nguyen", 23, 0)

b = Engineer("Clinton", "Akomea", 22, 0)

print(a)

print(a.email)

print(b)

print(b.email)
```

Output:

```
Lam Nguyen(age: 23)

Lam.Nguyen@techcomp.com

Clinton Akomea(age: 22)

Clinton.Akomea@techcomp.com
```

It is noted that the **pass** keyword is placed inside the body of the class Engineer as we don't want to do much of stuffs at this point. As we know, the **pass** statement is a null operation, so nothing happens when it executes. In other words, the class Engineer at this point just inherits from the superclass Employee and do nothing else.

As usual, the variable *a* is an Employee object with full of information passed in, so the first two lines of input just show us exactly what we knew and expected. On the other hand, the other variable *b* is an Engineer object, and its class does not have any information like the class Employee does. However, the only thing the Engineer class has is that it is the subclass of the Employee.

Therefore, despite having no information at this point, the class Engineer still inherits attributes and behavior methods from Employee, so *b*, an Engineer has every characteristic that *b* has: firstname, lastname, age, pay, and a readable printing "appearance". The output showed us clearly.

Now, consider a very interesting situation. Last week, the team Engineer in the company complete their job excellently, so the company decided to give them more 20% of their pay. In this case, we have to rewrite the calculatePay() method for only the class Engineer to make sure that all the engineers in the company get their extra pay. We will print out the pay of an Employee and an Engineer to check this.

```
class Employee:
    def __init__(self, firstname, lastname, age, pay):
        self.firstname = firstname
        self.lastname = lastname
        self.age = age
        self.pay = pay
        self.email = firstname + "." + lastname + "@techcomp.com"
    def __str__(self):
        return str(self.firstname) + " " + str(self.lastname) + "(age: " + str(self.age) + ")"
    def calculatePay(self):
        hours = input("Enter the number of hours: ")
        hourlyRate = input("Enter the hourly rate: ")
        self.pay = int(hours) * int(hourlyRate)
        return self.pay


class Engineer(Employee):
    def calculatePay(self):
        hours = input("Enter the number of hours: ")
        hourlyRate = input("Enter the hourly rate: ")
        self.pay = int(hours) * int(hourlyRate) * 1.2
        return self.pay
```

```
a = Employee("Lam", "Nguyen", 23, 0)

print(a)

print(a.pay)

a.calculatePay()

print(a.pay)

b = Engineer("Clinton", "Akomea", 22, 0)

print(b)

print(b.pay)

b.calculatePay()

print (b.pay)
```

Output:

Debug I/O	Python Shell	Messages	OS Commands	▼

Debug I/O (stdin, stdout, stderr) appears below   Options ▾

```
Lam Nguyen(age: 23)
0
Enter the number of hours: 40
Enter the hourly rate: 10
400
Clinton Akomea(age: 22)
0
Enter the number of hours: 40
Enter the hourly rate: 10
480.0
```

(The output was screenshotted from Wing IDE.)

From the output, it can be seen that both Employee and Engineer have the same amount of pay at the beginning, which is equal to 0. However, after the calculatePay() method is called and used, the pays of these two staff members are different although they both work 40 hours with the rate 10$ per hour. This is because the calculatePay() method was rewritten in the class Engineer with an extra of 20% for every engineer in the company. On the other hand, it is noted that although the calculatePay() method was changed, it still did not affect the Employee class as it just works in the Engineer class. That's why the output showed exactly what we expected: all the employee have the same pay, but all the engineers in the company get extra 20% of their pay.

We have learned how to modify a method in a subclass to solve salary problem in the company. Now it is time to try changing attributes so that every class has appropriate details of staff members. To be more detailed, the Engineer Department should have one more attribute called area as there are many types of engineers in the company such as software engineer, hardware engineer or security engineer.

However, our Employee class right now just accepts firstname, lastname, age, and pay. If we want to keep attributes from Employee class as well as pass in an area of engineering, we have to handle this situation by using super().__init__ technique, which is shown below:

```python
class Employee:
    def __init__(self, firstname, lastname, age, pay):
        self.firstname = firstname
        self.lastname = lastname
        self.age = age
        self.pay = pay
        self.email = firstname + "." + lastname + "@techcomp.com"

    def __str__(self):
        return str(self.firstname) + " " + str(self.lastname) + "(age: " + str(self.age) + ")"
```

```
    def calculatePay(self):

        hours = input("Enter the number of hours: ")

        hourlyRate = input("Enter the hourly rate: ")

        self.pay = int(hours) * int(hourlyRate)

        return self.pay


class Engineer(Employee):

    def __init__(self, firstname, lastname, age, pay, area):

        super().__init__(firstname, lastname, age, pay)

        self.area = area


b = Engineer("Clinton", "Akomea", 22, 0, "Software")

print(b)

print(b.area)
```

Output:

```
Clinton Akomea(age: 22)

Software
```

It can be seen that thanks in large part to the super().__init__ technique, the Engineer object still inherits attributes from Employee such as firstname, lastname or age without writing again lines of code. Besides, new attribute called *area* is passed in and we can check it by printing out b.area. The output is exactly what we expected.

In conclusion, object-oriented programming is a very broad topic. In this book, we just cover fundamental things that help you understanding what object-oriented programming is and how we can write our own classes effectively in different situations. Learning is never enough, so discover beyond this book as much as you can!

CHAPTER 11: ADVANCED TOPICS

• Recursion:

Recursion is a way of solving a problem by breaking a problem down into smaller sub-problems until you get to a problem that is small enough to be solved. In recursion, a function calls itself one or more times in its body. This kind of function is also called as recursive function. To write a recursive function, it is better to "think about what it does, rather than how it does". This is how we can write a recursive function:

1) Decide what name to give the function and what formal parameters the function needs to do its job.
2) Write the base case first. This is the non-recursive part. "I know how to do this, so I will do it and am out of here".
3) After completing base case, the function calls itself (recursive part). We must change the new formal parameter(s) in such a way as to get closer to the base case. We typically are making the new problem "smaller" than the current problem.
4) Recursive function often do not have a for loop or while loop.

We will understand more about recursive function via a function called revString() that reverses a String given.

This is a normal function revString() as we knew before:

```
def revString(aString):

    result = ""

    for i in range(len(aString)):

        result = aString[i] + result

    return result


print(revString("hello"))
```

Output:

olleh

This revString() function just simply concatenates every character of the given String in a backward way through a for loop. We can actually solve this problem by a recursive function.

To begin with, we decide the name of the function is revString(). After that, we have to determine the base case for our recursive function. This is an important step since the base case is like our first brick for the building. This is the first time you have created a base case, so let me help you get familiar with this. To create a base case, raise a question "What should the first case look like?" To be more detailed, if we work with a String, the first case should be an empty String. Similarly, if we work with a List, the first case should be an empty List.

In this case, we work with aString given, so we should start with an empty String – "". Remember the question "What should the first case look like?" What should be the reverse of an empty String? The answer is absolutely another empty String "". Next, we have to write the recursive case, which is the most challenging part of writing a recursive function. To get more idea about it, look at the code below:

```python
def revString(aStr):
    if aStr == "":
        return ""
    else:
        return revString(aStr[1:]) + aStr[0]
print(revString("hello"))
```

Output:

olleh

The recursive part did a great job. The statement revString(aStr[1:]) + aStr[0] may confuse you. Let me explain it step by step.

Given "hello" is aString to reverse, so aStr[0] in this code equal "h" at the beginning. So it can be understood that the result equals to revString("ello") + "h". Now, the function is called itself, so revString("ello") will return revString("llo") + "e". This process keeps going until each reach the base case. This is how it is processing:

Given:

"hello"

When the process goes to the base case:

➔ revString("ello") + "h"
➔ revString("llo") + "e"
➔ revString("lo") + "l"
➔ revString("o") + "l"
➔ revString("") + "o"
➔ "" + "o"

Return (Continue from the last line of the process above):

➔ "" + "o" = "o"
➔ "o" + "l" = "ol"
➔ "ol" + "l" = "oll"
➔ "oll" + "e" = "olle"
➔ "olle" + "h" = "olleh"

Now we reach the top, so the recursive function revString() returns "olleh" as expected.

We can also describe this process by the expression with parentheses as in Math:

return = ((((("" + "o") + "l") + "l") + "e") + "h")

= ((((("o" + "l") + "l") + "e") + "h")

= ((("ol" + "l") + "e") + "h")

= (("oll" + "e") + "h")

= ("olle" + "h")

= "olleh"

From this example, we can see that the base case starts everything as revString("") returns a specific value instead of calling a function itself. That's why we start adding up the String from "" + "o" = "o" and keeps going until no function is called anymore.

Remember:

- A recursive function must have its base case.
- A recursive function must change its state and move toward the base case.
- A recursive fucntion must call itself recursively.

❖ Coding Challenge:

Write recursive functions to solve these problems:

1) Write recursive function called sumList() to calculate the sum of all numbers in a List. For instance, fact([1,2,3,4]) would return 10, and fact([3,6,2,4]) would return 15.

2) Write recursive function called fact() to calculate the factorial number. In mathematics, the factorial of a non-negative integer n, denoted by n!, is the product of all positive integers less than or equal to n. For example:

0! = 1

1! = 1

2! = 1 x 2

3! = 1 x 2 x 3

4! = 1 x 2 x 3 x 4

5! = 1 x 2 x 3 x 4 x 5

Thus, fact(3) would return 6, and fact(5) would return 120.

(Solutions will be given on the next page)

Solutions to the Coding Challenge:

1) Solution to Question 1:

```
def sumList(aList):
  if len(aList) == 1:
     return aList[0]
  else:
     return aList[0] + sumList(aList[1:])


print(sumList([1,2,3,4]))
print(sumList([3,6,2,4]))
```

2) Solution to Question 2:

```
def fact(n):
  if n == 0:
     return 1
  else:
     return n * fact(n-1)


print(fact(3))
print(fact(5))
```

After two coding challenges, you may get more familiar with Recursion. All the recursive functions we discussed so far called themselves just one time in their body. Sometimes, recursive function actually can call itself more than one time in a statement. It's the Fibonacci number case.

Fibonacci numbers are a series of numbers in which each number is the sum of the two preceding numbers. This is a series of Fibonacci numbers:

1, 1, 2, 3, 5, 8, 13, 21, 34, 55, 89, ...

It can be seen that in the Fibonacci series, the first Fibonacci number is 1, the second number is 1, the third number is 2, the fourth one is 3 and so on... Let's call n is the position in the series and F(n) is the Fibonacci number at that position. This is the table that demonstrate this idea:

n	1	2	3	4	5	6	7	8	9	10
F(n)	1	1	2	3	5	8	13	21	34	55

Write recursive function called recursiveFib(n) to return a Fibonacci based on the given position. For instance, recursiveFib(5) would return 5, and recursiveFib(10) would return 55.

Try your best first before looking at the solution below.

And this is the recursive function to find the Fibonacci number:

```
def recursiveFib(n):
    if n == 1 or n == 2:
        return 1
    else:
        return recursiveFib(n-1) + recursiveFib(n-2)


print(recursiveFib(5))
print(recursiveFib(10))
```

Output:

5
55

The output is perfectly as expected. From this code above recursiveFib(5) equals to the sum of recursiveFib(4) and recursiveFib(3). We can demonstrate the idea of this code as follows:

recursiveFib(5) = recursiveFib(4) + recursiveFib(3)

recursiveFib(4) = recursiveFib(3) + recursiveFib(2)

recursiveFib(3) = recursiveFib(2) + recursiveFib(1)

Go from bottom up, we can see that recursiveFib(2) and recursiveFib(1) are base cases and they are both equal to 1. Therefore:

recursiveFib(3) = 1 + 1 = 2

recursiveFib(4) = 2 + 1 = 3

recursiveFib(5) = 3 + 2 = 5

That's why recursiveFib(5) equals to 5, and so does recursiveFib(10).

However, now the question is "What is the recursiveFib(106) ?"

Do not try it! Your computer may get in trouble. It is estimated that with this recursive function, you will find the 36th Fibonacci number more than minute. Even worse, computing recursiveFib(106) would take us more than 31 000 years as this function has exponential running time.

So what can we do to solve this Fibonacci problem more effectively?

• Memoization:

Memoization is a useful technique that can solve the Fibonacci problem smoothly. It is a smart technique used in computing to speed up programs. The strategy is memorizing the calculation results received from function calls. If a function call with the same parameters is used, the previously stored results can be used again instead of evaluating again unnecessary calculations. In Python, we use Dictionary to store results.

For example:

```
memo = {}
def recursiveFib(n):
    if n in memo:
        return memo[n]
    if n == 1:
        memo[1] = 1
        return 1
    if n == 2:
        memo[2] = 1
        return 1
    val = recursiveFib(n-1) + recursiveFib(n-2)
    memo[n] = val
    return val

print(recursiveFib(106))
```

Output:

```
635630699300684593037
```

This is amazing! So 635630699300684593037 is the 106th Fibonacci number. This memorization technique helps as the function now works more effectively. This is because instead of calling recursiveFib() function again and again, memorization technique just get the result from the list created at the beginning to continue. This saves a lot of time.

To be more detailed, you might still remember that without the memoization technique, to calculate recursiveFib(5), we have to calculate recursiveFib(4) and recursiveFib(3). To calculate recursiveFib(4), we have to calculate recursiveFib(3) one more time. Now, you can see our code just evaluate a calculation again and again. If the recursive process is big, this repetition is really bad because a lot of functions() are called many times. That's why recursiveFib(106) can get your computer in trouble.

On the other hand, with the Dictionary called memo declared, we just can get the value stored in it before instead of recalculate it again and again. That's how memoization speed up our program significantly.

• Linked Lists:

In Computer Science, data sequences can be organized in different ways. Unlike normal Python List we mentioned before in chapter 4, a **linked list** in Computer Science is a data structure consisting of a series of separated nodes which together represents a sequence.

Under the simplest form, each node is composed of 2 parts: data value and a reference (in other words, a **link**) to the next node in the sequence; more complex variants add additional links.

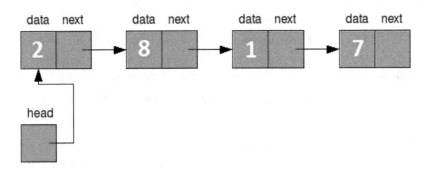

Comparison:

	List	**Linked List**
• Types:	dynamic array	doubly link
• Get(index):	O(1)	O(n)
• Insert:	O(n)	O(1)
• Remove:	O(n)	O(n)
• Good for:	store & access data	manipulate data

What is Node?

Again, each node consists of two pieces: the data associated
with the node and a link to the next node. This is the node class that shows node's characteristics that we have learned so far:

```
class Node:
    def __init__(self, item, pre = None, nex = None):
        self.item = item
        self.pre = pre
        self.nex = nex
    def getItem(self):
        return self.item
    def getNext(self):
        return self.nex
    def setItem(self,item):
        self.item = item
    def setNext(self,nex):
        self.nex = nex
    def __str__(self):
        return "Node(" + str(self.item) + "," + str(self.nex) + ")"
    def __repr__(self):
        return "Node(%s, %s)" % (repr(self.item), repr(self.nex))

nodeA = Node(4,None,5)
print(nodeA)
print(nodeA.getItem())
print(nodeA.getNext())
```

Output:

```
Node(4,5)
4
5
```

A Node object is created with two pieces: data value and a reference to the next node. Therefore, Node(4,5) means the item carried by this Node is 4, and the next Node has the data value of 5. Therefore, the output is as expected.

The class Node above is created just for making separated nodes, so we need to write a LinkedList class to connect these nodes as a chain.

```
class LinkedList:

    def __init__(self):

        self.head = None


    def __str__(self):

        s = ""

        node = self.head

        if node != None:

            while node.nex != None:

                s += "[" + str(node.item) + "]"

                node = node.nex

            s += "[" + str(node.item) + "]"

        return s
```

Now, this constructor allows you to create a Linked List with a readable form [node][node][node]...

Next, to see Nodes with values linked in the list, we write an add() method to add Nodes to the LinkedList created. In LinkedList, the first item added to the list will eventually be the last node on the linked list as every other item is added ahead of it. For example, if we want to add 2 to a newly-created LinkedList, then your list should become [2] now. After that, adding 8 to that List will return [8][2], not [2][8] because the new item is supposed to put ahead of the list. Therefore, if we want to put 2, 8, 1, 7 to our LinkedList, the LinkedList after that should contains

[7][1][8][2]. Now, let's try your best to write that add() method before looking at the code below to check it:

```
def add(self, item):
    node = Node(item)
    if self.head == None:
        self.head = node
    else:
        node.nex = self.head
        node.nex.pre = node
        self.head = node
```

First, to add a Node to a Linked List, we have to create and have a Node in our hand, so the statement node = Node(data) simply does that job. We use the if statement here for two different cases: when our LinkedList is empty and when it's not. When the LinkedList is empty, the head of this List is simply just the node we just added because it is the first Node of the List. Otherwise, the head of LinkedList at that time now becomes the next part of the new Node, and the part that comes before that part (the old head) now is the Node itself. Finally, of course the new head is just the Node put in because it is put ahead of the Linked List as we mentioned before. This part is kind of confusing, so take your time to think about it carefully. This is the images of how the process works. Hope that helps.

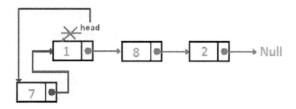

To see how the linkedlist changes everytime we put a new item, we can check the process by this following code:

```
mylist = LinkedList()

mylist.add(2)

print(mylist)

mylist.add(8)

print(mylist)

mylist.add(1)

print(mylist)

mylist.add(7)

print(mylist)
```

This will show:

```
[2]
[8][2]
[1][8][2]
[7][1][8][2]
```

The add() method written before returned [7][1][8][2] after we put 2, 8, 1, and 7 to the newly-created LinkeList. First of all, we created an empty Linked List called mylist and then added 2 to this newly-created LinkedList object, so mylist should become [2] now. After that, adding 8 to this List will return [8][2], not [2][8] because the new item is supposed to put ahead of the list as the picture described above. Therefore, because we put 2, 8, 1, 7 respectively to mylist – a LinkedList object created, the output shown is [7][1][8][2] as we expected.

Practice more with Linked List by writing a remove() and search() methods for your LinkedList class. The remove() method is supposed to get rid of the node you want to delete in the chain of nodes, while the search() method is made for checking whether a Node is in the LinkedList or not. This time the solutions are not given, so be creative and confident with your work. Good luck!

• Be a good coder!

It is not quite hard and easy as well to be a good coder. It is always true that "practice makes perfect!" Coding may be scary at the beginning, but when you get familiar with it, you will feel much better. Sometimes coding is overwhelming due to numerous lines of code or ambiguous syntaxes. Don't worry as we all are on the same boat and every talented programmer used to feel the same at the beginning. Be confident in yourself!

Now, this is tips that helps you during your journey to be a good coder:

1) Name variables that make sense!

Naming a variable plays a crucial role in coding. Although writing a number of different programs, many of us still underestimate the role of naming a variable. A variable name that makes sense absolutely helps programmer a lot in big projects. A good variable name is not only readable but also clear in meaning. For example, to name a function that check whether a number is a prime number or not, we should name it isPrime() instead of naming it checkANumber() or thefunctionthatcheckanumberisprimeornot(). The checkANumber() simply doesn't carry enough information of the function, while the latter name is just too long and too complicated to handle. On the other hand, isPrime() is very convenient to call anywhere in the big project or inside another function.

2) Break the big problems into smaller pieces!

Don't panic when you look at a huge problem. I know this is one of the most challenging tip to practice, but keep practicing will make you get more familiar with breaking big problems into suitably smaller pieces. The last coding challenge in chapter 9 is a prominent example: Write a program to create a new file that collect every word in the text file, how many times that word appears in the text, and lines containing that words. It is clear that there are a bunch of different problems to tackle in this project. First, think about how to collect every different words from the story without non-alphabetical characters. Second, think about how to count how many time a specific word appears in the text. Third, think about how we can know which lines that word appears. Finally, find way to write down all of our work to a new text file. That's how we break a huge problems into pieces.

3) Get used to with Debugging!

Programming is a complex process, so errors, which are also called bugs, are inevitable. The process of tracking them down and correcting them is called debugging.

There are three kinds of errors in a program: syntax errors, semantic errors, and runtime errors. Distinguishing between them helps coders track bugs down more quickly.

Syntax are rules or structures of a program that we have to follow. For example, the for loop requires a colon at the end and if we forgot to put it on, we made a syntax error.

A semantic error happens in your program when it runs successfully without any error message, but your program just does the wrong thing. For example, we write a program and expect the output to be 5, but the result we get is 6. There is no error to hint us which parts we did wrong like syntax errors. Our program just does wrong as the meaning of the program (its semantics) is wrong. Fixing semantic errors can be tricky because you have to go back and look at the logic of your program and trying to figure out what it is doing.

If a syntax error happens when Python can't understand what you are saying, then a run-time error happens when Python understands what you are saying, but runs into trouble when following your instructions. In other words, a runtime error is a program error that occurs while the program is running.

Setting regular break points in your IDE significantly supports you in debugging.

4) Visit Stack Overflow!

It is fun to know that Stack Overflow is the home of programmers. I can tell you that almost 90 percent of programmers used to click onto a link from Stack Overflow. This is where you can ask for help from other programmers, help other coders who need your help, and find knowledge that you are looking for. For example, if you remember the split() method to convert a String into a List, but you cannot remember and don't know how to convert a List back to a String, ask and visit Stack Overflow!

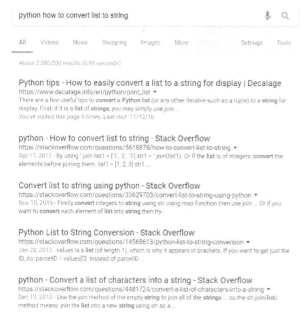

Thanks to our sweet home, now we know that the join() method is used to convert a List into a String. As a programmer, you may visit Stack Overflow a lot especially during the time we just started learning to code. Remember Stack Overflow is the home of us.

Index